I0519031

Phorgotten No More

Glimpses of the African-American presence in Phillipsburg, NJ

1777-2021

by
Wayne C. Sherrer

First Edition

Cover design by Gayle F. Hendricks
Cover photo by Reinhold Radke and used by permission
Phillipsburg High School yearbook photos used by permission.

Copyright © 2024 by Wayne C. Sherrer

Library of Congress Cataloging-in-Publication Data
Sherrer, Wayne, 1951-
Phorgotten No More: Glimpses of the African-American Presence in Phillipsburg, NJ 1777-2021 / Wayne C. Sherrer

ISBN-13: 978-1-957863-21-4
1. African-Americans-New Jersey-History 2. New Jersey-History

Notice: The information in this book is true and complete to the best of our knowledge. The capitalization of Black and white in regard to people conforms to AP style guidelines.

Printed in the United States

For the town of Phillipsburg
lest its history be forgotten.

Table of Contents

Foreword

The history of a community is found in its residents, its buildings, customs and foods. Phillipsburg is no exception. We reminisce about the cheeseburgers sold at Toby's Cup, savor Jimmy's hot dogs, recall the thin-crust pizza sold in corner stores and cherish our memories of the Key City Diner. Friday nights in the Fall means football, as does Thanksgiving when we take on the Rovers at Lafayette College. The Victorian buildings on South Main Street share a history along with the concrete homes built by Thomas Edison in Valley View.

But it is the people who came, stayed, returned and remember, who make Phillipsburg home, and why Phorgotten No More by Wayne Sherrer is important. Sherrer contributes to a deeper understanding of Phillipsburg through its examination of the role of its Black citizens. Historically, the population was small. The recognition of their past contributions creates opportunity for greater inclusion in the present.

Jobs brought people to the banks of the Delaware. My paternal Phillipsburg ancestors settled on Montana Mountain during the Revolutionary War, and my maternal Irish ancestors were part of the significant Irish migration to the banks of the Delaware in the late 1890s. They were not unique as the late 19th and early 20th century also saw significant growth in the Italian and German communities. So it should come as no surprise that African-Americans also migrated to Phillipsburg.

Why? Jobs. Jobs multiplied on the Morris and Delaware canals and the railroads, jobs expanded at the foundry and as Ingersoll-Rand and Baker Chemical grew and grew. By working hard and long and by saving, small businesses were launched. Second and third-generations saw their children go to college and return home as doctors, lawyers and teachers.

Historical knowledge such as that provided by Wayne Sherrer can guide policymakers and community leaders in making decisions that are sensitive to the community's heritage and needs. It helps in creating development plans that respect the past while aiming for a better future. Historians like Sherrer are needed to quilt incidents and issues together into a historical garment with a unifying message. The knots have to be tied together with data for events to make sense.

Acknowledging a community's history also fosters empathy and understanding among its members. It encourages respect for diverse perspectives and experiences, promoting a more inclusive and tolerant society. As a journalist for the Newark Star-Ledger and now as a faculty member at the University of Mississippi, that has been my quest such that I argue good journalism requires diverse sources, stories and staff. The same can be said for a municipality, in that a community needs diverse people contributing to the conversation, for workers and stories to thrive.

Learning about the past challenges overcome by a community can also inspire resilience and determination during present difficulties. It shows that overcoming adversity is part of the community's narrative and can provide hope for the future. We know that all too well—Friday night under the lights taught us all that lesson.

Kathleen Woodruff Wickham, Ed.D

Professor of Journalism
University of Mississippi
Phillipsburg High School, Class of 1967

Author of:
James Meredith: Breaking the Barrier.
Yoknapatawpha Press, 2022.

We Believed We Were Immortal: Twelve Reporters Who Covered the 1962 Integration Crisis at Ole Miss, preface by Bob Schieffer, Yoknapatawpha Press, 2017.

Acknowledgements

This story could not have been told without the unheralded work of the men and women in families, newspaper publications and in government offices who recorded and/or preserved the information collected for this volume. Although much was lost, including nearly every issue of the newspapers published in Phillipsburg prior to 1926, the outstanding collection of Easton newspapers, preserved by the Easton Area Public Library, was an invaluable resource.

My special thanks go to Sharon Gothard in the Marx Local History Room of that library. Our mutual interest in documenting Black residents on both sides of the Delaware River meant new primary sources were shared as either of us discovered them. This work was also made possible by the offices of Warren and Sussex counties, the collections of the New Jersey State Library in Trenton, the archives of the Alexander Library of Rutgers University, and the acquisitions of the Phillipsburg Area Historical Society.

I owe a debt of gratitude to the members of the Writers Group at the Phillipsburg Free Public Library for their feedback. My editor, Angel Ackerman, did a masterful job highlighting where clarification or other revisions were needed. Any errors of fact or interpretation are mine alone. My greatest thanks are to my wife and children for their indulgence of the countless hours I spent seeking the information and then compiling it into its current format.

Introduction

While president of the Phillipsburg Area Historical Society, I began researching and writing a detailed book on aspects of the town's history which had been overlooked in previous accounts. One of those subjects was the story of the town's Black population. The absence of a single photograph of a Black resident among the numerous pictures in the 1961 town centennial volume (William Dorsey of the 8-ball printers was an Easton resident) and a lone sentence in the town's 1911 Golden Jubilee booklet have given the false impression that there never was a Black population in town until recent times.

The larger book's chapter unveiling centuries of Phillipsburg's Black history kept expanding as my research progressed. I realized that the chapter deserved to be an entire book devoted to that single topic. The absence of local Black institutions and the loss of Phillipsburg's nineteenth century newspapers meant that a great deal of that history is irretrievable.

However, there is a substantial body of surviving information which had never been assembled. This book introduces some people who were scarcely noticed and quickly forgotten, yet who played a role in our common heritage.

Since Phillipsburg began as a small settlement within Greenwich township and there was considerable movement back and forth between the two entities, some of the material presented here necessarily includes information about the Black population in the larger Greenwich community. The considerable traffic between Easton, Pa and Phillipsburg, NJ likewise is responsible for the inclusion of several Black families and institutions from Easton.

Some of this information may be difficult to accept: that prominent early Phillipsburg residents participated directly in the enslavement of people from Africa, and, less surprising, that racial discrimination persisted long after slavery's abolition.

Nevertheless, there are also reasons for amazement and civic pride. Official government records of the birth of Black babies between 1804 and 1823 predate birth certificates for other children by several decades. Several leading families in the area took the necessary legal action to secure the freedom of their slaves. Black home ownership in town began in 1837. A Black couple in 1839 inherited real estate through the will of a white clergyman. Black children attended school as early as 1850.

Black residents of this community served admirably in the military during the Civil War. Black residents in town were registered to vote as soon as the 15th amendment to the constitution went into effect and were escorted to the polls for their first voting experience in 1870. A Black man, Mahlon Chamberlin, ran for political office in 1881 on a major party ticket. Not only was he one of New Jersey's earliest Black candidates, he was almost victorious.

This volume is far from a comprehensive history of the Black experience in Phillipsburg or the final word on the subject. I invite others to expand upon this initial effort. This book is rather a recognition of the town's diversity from its earliest years, an account of some of the contributions Black residents have made to the town, and an embrace of all who have called Phillipsburg their home.

Wayne Sherrer, December 2023

Chapter 1

Pre-Civil War

"The first interment in this cemetery [Phillipsburg Cemetery] was made in 1844, when a colored child, which had fallen in the sand-pit, died of its injuries and was buried in Mr. Roseberry's wheat field."[1]

This sentence in the Charter Jubilee program of 1911 is the only reference to any Black person in Phillipsburg in any previously published chapter or book on the history of Phillipsburg. Some obvious questions arise: Where did the child come from? Why did the parents think Mr. Roseberry's wheat field was an appropriate place for the child's burial? And, perhaps most puzzling of all, why did Mr. Roseberry consent to that burial? A possible answer to some, not all, of these questions may be found by an examination of the surviving records of the earliest Black residents of the Phillipsburg area.

While Phillipsburg has long been a melting pot of various nationalities, the presence of Blacks in the community has been ignored in historical accounts. Unlike other immigrants, Africans did not choose to settle in the Phillipsburg area of their own free will. New Jersey was a colony and later, a state, in which slave-holding was legal.

At New Jersey's founding in 1664, English settlers were given 150 acres of land to get started – plus an additional 150 for each enslaved person they brought with them.[2] Slavery in New Jersey did not officially end until 1866, three years after the Emancipation Proclamation, which only freed slaves in the

---

[1]   *Historical Program, Charter Jubilee*, Phillipsburg, NJ 1911
[2]   Whitehead, William, *East Jersey under the Proprietary Governments* Newark, NJ: Martin R. Dennis, 1875, p. 38

states that had seceded from the Union. Documents reveal that some residents of Phillipsburg were participants in the business of African enslavement.

For example, on July 9, 1777 a Phillipsburg resident named Thomas Scott advertised a reward of six dollars for the return of Ben, his runaway Negro. Ben was described as 23-years-old, five-feet, seven-inches tall and lame in one of his legs and foot.[3] (It is worth noting that this was Ben's third advertised escape within thirteen months, but the first time Phillipsburg was mentioned.)

In a second example, George Taylor, signer of the Declaration of Independence, lived in Greenwich Township in 1779-80 while running the Greenwich Forge. The settlement of his estate in 1781 included the sale of two slaves: Tom and crippled Sam.

And the list goes on. The Greenwich estate of Edward Hunt was settled in 1786 by his son's payment for the value of the slave Sambo. In another prominent Greenwich family, brothers Thomas and William Kennedy, were served by seven known slaves and by seven children of those slaves. A family Bible which preserved some of their names and dates, supplements the governmental records.[4]

St. James Lutheran Church recorded the birth and baptisms of two children born to slaves before 1790. The Federal census of 1800 counted 64 slaves in Greenwich Township (which included the village of Phillipsburg). One sign of slavery's acceptance are the records of manumissions (slave emancipations) by the Rev. William B. Sloan, pastor of Old Greenwich Presbyterian Church and by the Rev. Garner A. Hunt, pastor of Oxford Presbyterian Church.

---

[3]   Pennsylvania Gazette *NJ Archives Second Series*, vol I, p. 424
[4]   See Appendix A

According to 1798 legislation, slaves between the ages of 21 and 40 could be set free by their owner via a writ of manumission. After an inspection by two overseers of the poor and two justices of the peace determined that each was of sound mind and capable of obtaining his or her own support, a judge in the Court of Common Pleas ratified the emancipation. The law also mandated that those writs of manumission be recorded by the county clerk. The earliest recorded manumission in Greenwich Township did not occur until 1812.

In 1804, the New Jersey Assembly paved the way for the eventual abolition of slavery in the state. The 1804 law mandated that county clerks record every child born to a slave in their respective counties. Those children were deemed legally free, but were considered servants of their mother's owner until a female child reached 21 years of age or a male child reached 25 years. The county registration of birth ensured that the ages of those who reached adulthood were accurate. Sussex and Warren County records provide the names of 27 Black babies, along with the names of their enslaved mothers and slave owners, who were born in Greenwich between 1804 and 1823.[5] Slavery was officially abolished in New Jersey in 1846.

At the close of the 18th century the vast majority of the land within the boundaries of present day Phillipsburg was owned by four families: the Geassers, Beidlemans, Feits and Roseberrys. Those aforementioned governmental records, some church records and other sources reveal that all four of those families owned slaves.

On the southern end of town from Center Street through the Huntington neighborhood of Pohatcong Township were the farm and gristmills of Valentine Beidleman. He manufactured flour for the Philadelphia market and through his business

---

[5]   See appendix A

dealings in that place he had access to the slave market in that city. The information on the Beidleman slaves provides the earliest birth dates of Black residents of Phillipsburg. Among the records of St. James Lutheran Church is one for the baptism of Susanna, who was the daughter of Richmond and Jane, both slaves of Valentine Beidleman. Susanna was born on June 29, 1787 and baptized on September 15, 1788, with Barbara Beidleman as her sponsor. Five other slaves and six of their indentured children are identified by name in birth records or manumission records as being the property of Valentine Beidleman or his sons.[6]

George von Giesche (aka George Geasser) built a home on Fourth Street north of Broad Street. He owned 700 acres north of the bridge over the Delaware River. His will directed that "Pompey" should not be sold, but rather that he should choose whichever son he desired as his master.[7] The chapter on Lopatcong township by David Schwartz in the History of Warren County, published in 1881, mentions that Mr. von Giesche had owned several slaves.[8] In a 1936 newspaper account during the town's Diamond Jubilee, a descendant of the Geassar-Howell family revealed:

> Several slaves were kept and for years their graves might have been seen on the plantation near the present site of the Canister Company.[9]

The area from Hudson Street to Center Street and from Roseberry Street to the Delaware River was the property of the Roseberry family. A newspaper account after the 1893 death of Mrs. William Mackey Lovell, a Roseberry descendant, reported that in 1797 John Roseberry had given to his son Michael 228 acres of land (a portion of the 730 acres he

---

6   See Appendix A and Appendix C
7   George Geasser will *NJ Archives First Series*, vol XL, p. 137
8   Snell, James P., ed. *History of Warren County*, 1881, pg 680.
9   "Oldest Residence in Phillipsburg," *Phillipsburger*, July 30, 1936

distributed to his four sons) in recognition of his 21st birthday. The land stretched from Hudson Street to Andover Furnace, between the river and John Feit's land. The gift also included two slaves, a colored man and woman.

We find that on the 18th day of March, 1797, the year that Michael, his youngest child, came of age, John Roseberry gave to his four sons, John, Joseph, William and Michael, 730½ acres of land. Michael got the 228 acre plantation mentioned above. Shortly after this event John, the father, sets out in a recorded paper a deed that he had not made Michael even with his other five children, and then proceeded to make him equal. Of these five were two daughters, Hannah and Katharine. John bought for Henry Winter, Jr.,—the Lieu. Henry Winter that served in Capt. Jacob Winter's company in the first regiment in the Revolution, husband of Hannah Roseberry—about 300 acres of land in Harmony township, which the Ameys now own. Just how he made Katharine equal I am unable to say, as she went with her husband to Somerville, N. J. Anyway, in this paper he says that he made the five equal, and then Michael, the sixth child, is made equal to each of the other five. Michael was just twenty-one years of age, owning that splendid river flat lying between Hudson street and Andover Furnace, the river and John Feit's and Kinney's containing 228 acres with two slaves, a colored man and woman, wearing silver spurs, silver knee buckles, and silk stockings. His oil painting shows him to have been a good looking and well dressed man, tall and broad shouldered. With his blue eyes and well shaped head and face he looked like an English country gentleman.

Newspaper clipping in collection of Phillipsburg Area Historical Society

7

Michael's wife, Margaret Mackey, entered their marriage with her own slave, Sally. That slave may have been the 28 year old slave named Sarah whom Michael Roseberry freed on December 10, 1822. Upon examination, it was determined that she was of sound mind and not under any bodily incapacity. [so she would not be in danger of becoming a ward of the public]. Thomas Stewart, Judge of the Court of Common Pleas, then ratified her manumission.[10]

In 1749, John Feit purchased about 700 acres east of Roseberry Street. The 1830 US Census reveals that Paul Feit still had a male slave in his possession at that late date. The Feit property was sold to Ingersoll-Rand in 1902 for their new manufacturing complex. However, before the property changed hands, Mr. Feit's descendants arranged for the disinterment of 11 slaves bodies from the premises and the proper reburial of them in the cemetery of St. James Lutheran (Straw) Church.[11]

How does all of this apply to the burial of that unfortunate Black child in 1844? According to the Hon. Ralph Voorhees, "almost every family in former days had places on their farm where they buried their colored dead."[12] The evidence from the Geasser and Feit properties indicates this practice was followed in Greenwich Township. A plausible explanation for the burial in 1844 of the unnamed Black child in Mr. Roseberry's wheat field is that the site was likely the final resting place of the Roseberry slaves.

Rather than a burial in the old Brainard Street cemetery with the dead of Phillipsburg's white families, the dead child was laid to rest beside others who shared her heritage and may have been her ancestors. Sadly, the earliest records of

---

[10] See Appendix C for full text of her manumission
[11] See Appendix E
[12] Quoted in Snell, James,ed. *History of Hunterdon & Somerset Counties*, Philadelphia: Everts & Peck, 1881, p. 104

Phillipsburg Cemetery were destroyed by fire and the child's name has been lost forever. However, that child's interment insured that the subsequent Phillipsburg Cemetery would be an integrated burial ground more than a decade before the Civil War.

Phillipsburg was home to some anti-slavery sentiment. Its presence on the Underground Railroad is explained by Phillipsburg's status as a transportation hub.[13] A map in The New Jersey Underground Railroad Project's 2020 booklet *Steal Away, Steal Away* indicated that a building which served as a station on the Underground Railroad was still standing in Phillipsburg. Their report to the state legislature identified that building as the former Eagle Hotel on Chambers Street at Stockton Street.[14]

It is fitting that in 2006 a Black woman named Sandra Edwards purchased the building. Until 2017, the Edwards Learning Center offered tutoring, test preparation and technology training to students. The former Springtown Stagecoach Inn on Route 519 in Pohatcong Township was also identified as a station in the booklet.[15]

---

[13] Switala, *Underground Railroad*, p. 67.
[14] Appendix 6, NJ Historical Commission, New Jersey Underground Railroad Project, *Report to the State Legislature*, Trenton 2002, p. 34
[15] Wiles & Wonkeryor, *Steal Away, Steal Away, p. 9.*

Former Eagle Hotel

Chapter 2

Civil War to 1920

On the eve of the Civil War, Phillipsburg's future looked promising. Factories had been built and enlarged to produce iron and brass products. Railroad lines connected the town south to Trenton, east to Elizabeth and west to Pennsylvania's anthracite coal region. Hotels catered to the growing number of travelers through the town's boundaries. Employed primarily in the hospitality sector, the town's Black population was expecting to enjoy the benefits of the town's growing prosperity. And then the war began.

Black residents of Phillipsburg and Greenwich joined their white neighbors in military service during the Civil War. Black men were exempt from the draft until The Enrollment Act of March 1863 required their registration. When state officials in New Jersey were slow to implement the law, impatient local Black men went out of state to enlist. Frank and Thomas Duncan, Alfred James, James Miller, James Spruell and Nelson Truax enlisted in Pennsylvania; Daniel Prime enlisted in Massachusetts; and brothers Alexander and Hezekiah Beidleman joined the U.S. Navy in New York. The war's end and the post war amendments to the United States Constitution gave Black residents renewed hope for a better life.

While New Jersey's first state constitution in 1776 had theoretically given property-owning women and free Blacks the right to vote, that right had been withdrawn by the state legislature in 1807. Two months after the ratification of the Fifteenth Amendment to the United States Constitution, Phillipsburg's first Black voters cast their ballots on April 11, 1870 in local elections. They missed being among the first Black voters in the state by two weeks because Black residents of Perth Amboy voted on March 31 in a special election held in that city alone.)[16] In a peculiar twist, newspaper accounts of the town's very first Black voter identify the white man who escorted him to the polls, but do not report the name of the voter himself.[17]

Eleven years later, a Black man, Mahlon Chamberlin, was the Republican candidate for Pound Keeper, the government official responsible for the feeding and care of stray livestock, in the town's first ward. Although only nine Black men were eligible to vote in that ward, Mahlon received 145 votes, yet lost by six votes. He was surely one of the first Black major party candidates for public office in New Jersey.[18]

The DeMotts and the Duncans were the families with the longest Black Philllipsburg residency in the 1800's. Detailed biographies in Chapter Four discuss their stories at length. Both Thomas DeMott and Joseph Duncan were hostlers, who tended to the horses of travelers spending time in Phillipsburg hotels. Other Black hostlers in the town were Thomas Johnson, Nelson Truax, Elias Anderson, and Charles Robinson. In addition, those hotels had other Black employees: barbers Daniel Prime, Robert Welsh and Rhodes C. Black; cooks Patty Rosin and George Lambert; waiters James Rosin and Adam Forman; servant Sidney Black; and wash woman Jane Forman.

By 1880, a number of women engaged in the laundry business: Elizabeth and Martha Steppler, Jane DeMott, Anna Smalley, and Sarah, Catherine and Agnes Chamberlin.

Census records record that many of the Black men and women in Phillipsburg and Greenwich Township were able to read and write. Children in the DeMott, Wells, Emery, Duncan and

---

[16] "Local and State News," *Evening Free Press*, Easton, PA, April 1, 1870, p.3
[17] *Evening Free Press*, April 13, 1870, p.3
[18] See his biography in Chapter 4.

Spruell families attended school in town, while children of the Furman, James, Innes, Huff, Sill and Freeman families went to school outside town in Greenwich Township

Some of Phillipsburg's Black families were active in Easton's Lutheran churches, notably St. John's Lutheran, Christ Lutheran and the First Colored Evangelical Lutheran Church. Others were married or had children baptized at Easton's First Methodist, First Presbyterian and Trinity Episcopal churches. Finally, in the 1880s weddings of Black couples were performed by clergy at St. Luke's Episcopal and First Methodist in Phillipsburg.[19]

Surprisingly, the Black population of Phillipsburg declined in number through the second half of the 19th century. The 32 Black residents who were recorded in the 1900 census were significantly fewer than the 45 enumerated in 1860, despite the town's growth from 3748 to 10,058 inhabitants. And while 34 of the 45 Black residents in 1860 had been born in New Jersey (nine of them under the age of ten), only four of the 25 adults in 1900 were New Jersey natives. Ten of the 25 had been born in Virginia, two in North Carolina, two in Delaware, two in New York and five in Pennsylvania. This chart shows how the Black presence in Phillipsburg changed during the first 50 years after the town's 1861 incorporation, with a spike before the Golden Jubilee in 1911, followed by an immediate decline.

---

[19]   See Appendix B

13

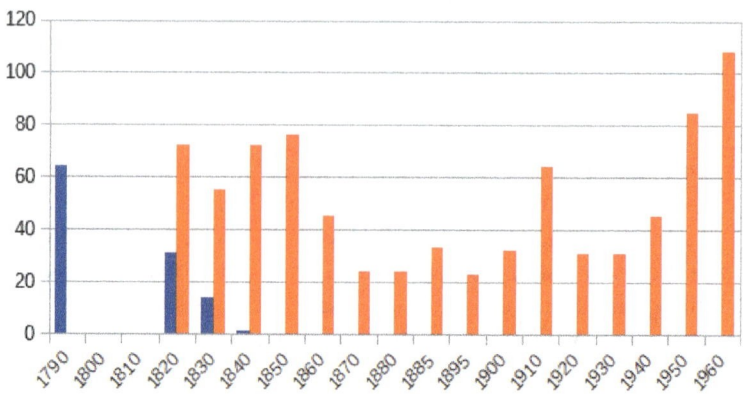

Enslaved (blue bars) and free (red bars) Black persons in Greenwich
Township through 1850 and in Phillipsburg from 1860 to 1960

While the town grew substantially from 1850 to 1900, Blacks
as a percentage of the population became nearly invisible.

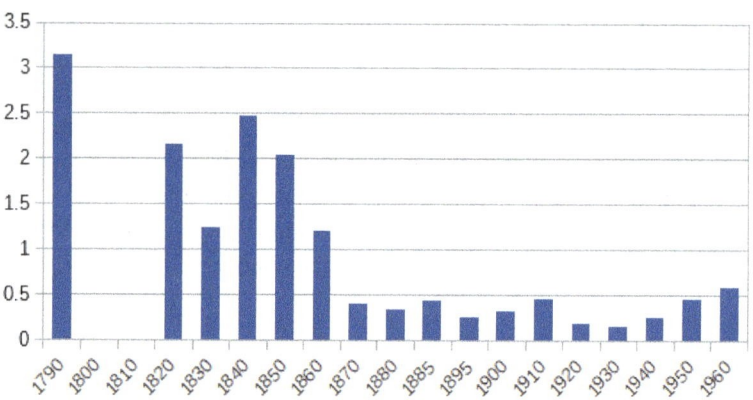

Black persons as a percentage of the total population of Greenwich
Township through 1850 and of Phillipsburg from 1860 to 1960

What factors can account for these statistics over more than
half a century? The first was simply a lack of critical mass.
The Black population of Phillipsburg was simply too small to
be self-sustaining. There were not enough Black residents to

14

establish local social or religious institutions. In contrast, temptingly across the river, Easton boasted a Colored Lutheran Church as early as 1866.[20] (There was overlap between the two communities. Rev. William Cornman pastored the First Colored Lutheran Church in Easton before becoming pastor of Grace Lutheran Church in Phillipsburg.) The Union African Methodist Episcopal Church of Easton organized in 1887. Shiloh Baptist separated from First Baptist of Easton in 1904 as another place for Black Christians to congregate.

Churches were not the only social center for Blacks available tin Easton, but non-existent in neighboring Phillipsburg. The Colored Drum Corps in Easton had formed by 1869. Easton also claimed a lodge of the Grand United Order of Odd Fellows, a fraternal organization for Blacks.

The small size of Phillipsburg's Black community meant that young Black adults seeking marriage partners had to look outside the town for possible candidates, and, as a result, often relocated (sometimes just across the river to Easton). Examples of 19th century marriage partners from distant locations include Ann DeMott's marriages to James Spruell from South Carolina and to Isaac Smalley from Canada, Mary Ellen Chamberlain's marriage to Edward Wilson from Louisiana, and Spencer Duncan's marriage to Carolinda Folks from Virginia. The Duncan family is the only Black family to be counted in Phillipsburg in every federal census from 1850 to 1900, while the DeMotts were present from 1830 to 1890. In 1870 the Black population in town was concentrated in just three families: the Duncan, DeMott and Wells families (20 of the 25 individuals).

A second factor affecting Black workers in Phillipsburg was the steady immigration of poor whites from Germany and

---

[20]   Easton's Colored Lutheran Church was organized in 1866 by Rev. D. W. Greenville and was affiliated with Christ Lutheran Church.

Ireland in the late nineteenth century, which proved stiff competition for both skilled and unskilled Blacks seeking employment. Black disappeared from jobs in the hospitality sector and found no welcome in the local factories during the 50 years of the town's industrialization from 1848 to 1898. Martin Freeman operated a courier service for Warren Manufacturing between their factory locations in Warren Glen and Riegelsville, but was not allowed to work inside the buildings. Not until 1900 do we see Black men at work in Warren Pipe foundry, Tippett and Wood Boiler Works or in the cement mill.

If the desire for spouses, work or participation in Black institutions supplied motivation for Black residents to leave Phillipsburg, the sheer number of transportation options in Phillipsburg provided the means for that desire to be pursued. Five railroads providing passenger and freight service to Phillipsburg (Jersey Central, Morris & Essex, Lehigh Valley, Lehigh & Hudson, and Bel-Del), three canals (Morris, Lehigh and Delaware), the Delaware River and the network of roads radiating from the town made it possible (even easy) to leave. While those same factors made it just as easy for other Blacks to enter the town, there was little inducement for them to remain in Phillipsburg. A visible sign of Black transience is the fact that Thomas DeMott and Henry Wells were the only Black residents to own real estate in the town between 1840 and 1940.

The final factor that impeded the growth of Phillipsburg's Black population was the existence of explicit and implicit racial prejudice against Black people. Although certainly not universal, racism was sufficiently widespread to influence the decision to remain or to move on. Before housing discrimination was outlawed in 1968, large sections of town had no Black renters or homeowners. However, live-in servants were acceptable.

During the first presidential campaign after the conclusion of the Civil War, a leaflet was distributed in Phillipsburg with the title "White Boys in Blue! Attention!"[21] It was an appeal by the White Soldiers' and Sailors' Union to support the candidacy of Horatio Seymour to be president of the United States. A key element of Seymour's platform was his opposition to Black equality and Black voting rights. The chairman of the local organization was local war hero Gen. Charles Heckman and its secretary was Charles Sitgreaves, Phillipsburg's first mayor and a member of the US House of Representatives during that election.

Interracial marriage was a recurring concern. An 1860 writer in the Easton Argus lamented:

> In all our experience as a journalist we have never been called upon to record so many cases of practical amalgamationism-- so many elopements of white women with black men, as have disgraced this country within the last five or six months. Almost every paper we open from the cities of the East or Northwest contains some new case of this character painful to read.[22]

When the Hon. Galusha A. Grow (24th Speaker of the U.S. House of Representatives) gave a commencement address at Lafayette College in 1868 that promoted intermarriage and the admission of Blacks to college, local newspapers reported that

> his performance was denounced as an outrage by all the faculty of the College, without an exception, by nearly all the students, by Gov. Pollock, by all the clergy and by every decent stranger and citizen who happened to be present.[23]

---

[21] A copy is in the Special Collections and Archives of the Alexander Library at Rutgers University, New Brunswick, NJ.

[22] *Easton Argus*, March 29, 1860

[23] *Easton Argus*, August 6, 1868

The following article in the *New Jersey Telegram*, whose name "More Miscegenation" already sets the racist tone for the piece, was published in Phillipsburg in 1892:

> Another white woman has shown to what degradation her sex can be drawn by being united in marriage to a Black man named Howard Prime of Easton. The ceremony was performed on Christmas eve at the residence of a colored woman in this city, the Rev. Smith, of Easton, officiating. This dominie seems to be doing a brisk business in marrying those of his color to white girls.[24]

But as the twentieth century dawned in the year 1900, there were signs in 1900 that change was in the air for Blacks in Phillipsburg. In December of 1900 the Twilight Social Club, organized under the leadership of Augustus A'Vant and Walter Lee, held a successful cakewalk in Ortygia Hall (the town's pre-eminent location at the time for indoor events).[25] The cakewalk was a dance originated by Black slaves on Southern plantations. According to Brook Baldwin, the cakewalk was intended "to satirize the competing culture of supposedly 'superior' whites." [26]

The 1900 census provides the first direct evidence of Blacks in the town's numerous factories. Of twelve adult men, four were employed in manufacturing. One was employed at Tippett and Wood Boiler Works and one at Warren Pipe Foundry, while two men worked in a cement mill (outside town).

More and more Black workers entered the manufacturing industries in Phillipsburg prior to the First World War. By

---

[24] "More Miscegenation," *New Jersey Telegram*, Phillipsburg, NJ January 3, 1892

[25] *Easton Daily Free Press*, 20 Dec 1900. p.3

[26] Baldwin, Brooke, "The Cakewalk: A Study in Stereotype and Reality"
Journal of Social History, vol. 15, p. 211

1910 there were seven Black men at the pipe foundry and three at the boiler works. Immigration from Europe was then restricted during the first world war, yet manufacturing boomed. The ensuing labor shortage led many New Jersey factories to recruit Black and white laborers from small towns and farms in southern states. In 1916 the Warren Pipe foundry hired additional Black employees and housed them in a company owned building on Sitgreaves Street. Upon receiving complaints from neighboring residents, the town's Director of Public Safety. Mr. Bates, inspected the premises, talked to Spellman Brown, the foundry's superintendent, about needed improvements, and reported his findings to the town commissioners. Mayor Frank Kneedler's response was blunt: "We don't want a lot of 'n****rs' to come here and create a nuisance in the town." [27]

NEGROES   HOUSED   THERE.

Mayor Declares "We Don't Want a Lot of 'Niggers' to Come Here and Create a Nuisance."

The Warren Foundry & Machine

His words headlined the newspaper account and the result was dramatic. By 1920, there were only three Black men left at the foundry and one at the boiler works. Families with young children fled the town as the Black population dropped from 64 in 1910 to only 28 in 1920. Some residents did not move far. Jennie Wilson and her children moved to Springtown, Pohatcong Township. Richard Dickerson and William Rosser took their families to Burlington, NJ. Others put more distance between themselves and Phillipsburg. By 1920 Daniel Dickerson and family had moved to Washington, DC. In 1910

---

[27]   "Negroes Housed There," *Easton Daily Express*, Easton, Pa, May 17, 1916, p. 6

there were 29 children under the age of 16, but 1920 recorded only six. The trend persisted through the following decade: only four children under the age of 16 in 1930, a single Black employee at the pipe foundry, only four of Phillipsburg's Black adults in 1930 had been town residents in 1920 and merely three of those adults had been born in New Jersey.

Mayor Kneedler's opinion was shared by a significant number of town residents. In June of 1927 and 1928, the local Ku Klux Klan women's auxiliary hosted entertainment for branches from other towns at Ortygia Hall, the same hall that hosted the Twilight Social Club nearly three decades earlier.[28]

Phillipsburg was not a regional anomaly in having residents with racist sentiments during that period. Hooded members of the Klan were photographed in Stewartsville's Memorial Day parade in 1925[29], while cross burnings occurred in Broadway, Washington, Hope (all NJ) and Easton, Pa[30]. The Washington Klavern was large enough and wealthy enough in 1924 to purchase the Cornish mansion, home of the late Senator Johnston Cornish, to serve as its headquarters. Members celebrated their purchase by burning a 50 foot high cross.[31] A crowd of about 1300 showed up New Year's Eve 1924 for the opening night of the four day dedication of the "Klan palace." The next two days saw 3000 people attending the festivities.[32]

---

[28]   "Klan Women Meet Here," *Easton Express*, June 14, 1928, p. 8
[29]   Greenwich Township Historical Society, *Through the Years* The Society: Greenwich, NJ, [1987?], pp 54-5
[30]   (Pa)"Fiery Cross on Mt. Ida," *Easton Express,* April 2, 1923, p 4.
[31]   "Celebrate New Home" *Washington Star,* November 27, 1924, p. 1
[32]   "Klan's Home is Dedikated" *Washington Star,* January 8, 1925, p.1

CONCLUSION

In the approximately 50 years between the Civil War and 1920, Black residents in Phillipsburg faced certain challenges in maintaining and expanding their numbers in the town. Since the town lacked social and religious institutions for these residents, they often had to move elsewhere to raise families. All residents, regardless of race, could easily travel because of Phillipsburg's geographic position as a transportation hub. As the Industrial Revolution and the First World War created more need for laborers and manufacturing, Black residents of Phillipsburg had to face rising racist attitudes which prompted many families to leave via the same roads that made Phillipsburg attractive in the first place.

Chapter 3

Post World War I

Mayor Kneedler's racist sentiments as noted in Chapter Two were hardly universal. In other instances, Black people contributed to the social and cultural richness of the town without hindrance especially in the era after the First World War. In 1921, the Tuskegee Institute Singers performed in Gospel Hall at Tyndall & Washington streets.[33] The following year the Hayes Colored Trio were highly praised for their renditions of classical songs and Negro folklore during the June Chautauqua.

Considering Phillipsburg's storied appreciation of athletic achievement, it is no surprise that sports played a leading role in the integration of the town's Black and white residents. Harry Case, Jr, the first Black graduate of Phillipsburg High School in 1929, blazed a trail on the field for the generations of Black student athletes who followed. Black stars on Phillipsburg teams were celebrated by team members, other students and townspeople, white and Black alike. Spectators flocked to North End field to see teams from the Negro Baseball Leagues, who were frequent visitors to Phillipsburg. During July 1934 alone, the local North End team played the Philadelphia Colored Stars, NY Black Yankees, Homestead Grays and Pittsburgh Crawfords.[34] Black All Stars who displayed their talents under the lights of Phillipsburg's North End field included Hall of Famers Satchel Paige, Josh Gibson, Cool Papa Bell, Buck Leonard, and Ray Dandridge.

---

[33] Notice in *Easton Express*, July 1, 1921
[34] *Easton Express* July 2, 8, 12, 18, 30 in 1934

Baseball autographed by Ray Dandridge[35]

It was time for another new beginning. In the Great Migration of the 20th century (1916-1970) about six million African-Americans moved from the rural South to urban centers in the Northeast, Midwest and West. As a manufacturing center and transportation hub, Phillipsburg was a direct beneficiary of this event. One of the first new families to settle in town was Esau and Rebecca Wallace. The Great Depression ushered in new Black immigrants to Phillipsburg. John Thornton, Cleveland Wooten and William Strickland joined the WPA road construction crews. They brought their families and stayed. The Williams and Flowers families joined the community after World War II as the number of Blacks in town steadily increased from 45 in 1940 to 85 in 1950 and 108 in 1960.

As mentioned earlier, Harry Case, Jr. from Pohatcong Township was in 1929 the first Black graduate of Phillipsburg High School. His Pohatcong cousins, Betty Martin (1933),

---

[35]   In the private collection of Richard Norton

James Martin (1934) and Carolyn Martin (1939) followed .
Also from Pohatcong were Geraldine (1942), Marie (1946)
and Elizabeth (1947) Freeman and Kenneth (1941) and Marion
(1944) Peterson. In 1946, Anna Wallace became the first
Black graduate of Phillipsburg High School who lived within
the town limits.

Later Black graduates included Robert Wooten (1956), Betty
Wilburn (1958), Roger Case (1958), Clyde Hataway (1960),
Eric Peterson (1960), Karen Peterson (1965), and Leon
Peterson (1968). The class of 1969 provided evidence that the
town's Black population was growing. The trio of Cynthia
Walden, Richard Williams and Charles Utley was the largest
group of Black students to receive diplomas in a single year.

Reinhold Radke photo of Mercer St. playground pool in 1963

Integration into the adult community was a slower process. The town's centennial in 1961 was observed by numerous men and women in chapters of Brothers of the Brush and Sisters of the Swish. These groups were formed by people who shared a workplace, a neighborhood, a school, a church, a tavern or some other social bond. During the yearlong celebration, the men grew beards and the women obtained 19th century dresses and bonnets. Many of the groups marched in the centennial parade, sometimes with floats they constructed. Among all the affinity groups in the centennial book, a single Black person was photographed. An Easton resident named William Dorsey joined his coworkers at Mack Printing in Wilson Borough as a member of the 8-ball Printers.

The town's demographic changes in the 1960s were not stress-free. Mayor Arthur Paini and *Free Press* editor Richard Reeves were elected to serve on the Easton-Phillipsburg Commission on Human Relations. That commission investigated housing and employment discrimination against minority groups in the two communities and also sought to uncover patterns of discrimination in public health, educational and recreational opportunities.

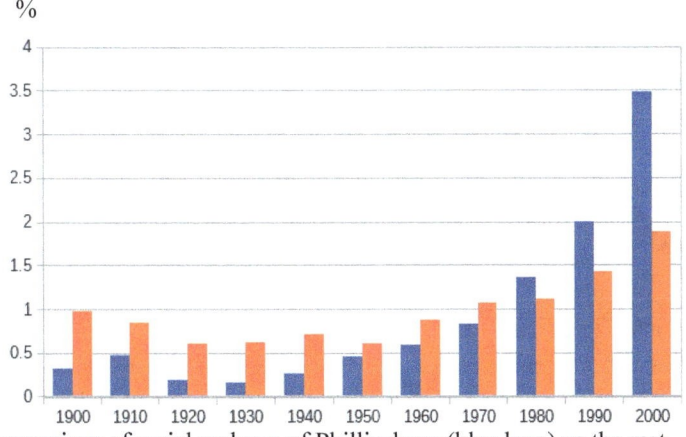

Comparison of racial makeup of Phillipsburg (blue bars) vs the rest of Warren County (red bars)

The federal Civil Rights Act of 1968 (known popularly as the Fair Housing Act) served as a catalyst for Phillipsburg's transition into a more racially diverse community. The Black population subsequently experienced robust growth: 146 in 1970, 224 in 1980, 313 in 1990 and 527 in 2000. In 1980, the proportion of Blacks in Phillipsburg (1.35%) finally exceeded the proportion in the rest of Warren County (1.11%).

In 1973, David C. Moore, Jr organized Grace Baptist Church to serve the town's growing Black population. Other initial trustees of the congregation were: Morris Shorter, Patrick Taylor and Betty Jones (all of Easton). Founding members included Leatha Chaney, Keturah Prescod, Ruth Bailey, Lucille G. Moore, Samuel Shelly, Nora Shelly, James Jordan, Cleveland Wooten, and Genean Roane. The congregation moved into the former First Baptist Church building on South Main Street and remained until about 2011.

In April 2010, Pastor Andre Thompson started the Citywide Church of God with Sunday School and worship services on Sunday afternoons in Westminster Presbyterian Church. Meanwhile, Enock Berluche Sr, a member of St. Philip & St. James' Roman Catholic Church, was ordained a permanent deacon in 1998. In addition to his parish duties, he is co-coordinator of African-American, Black and Caribbean Apostolate. In 2015 Gerard Jameson became pastor of Wesley United Methodist Church (the first Black pastor of a traditionally white congregation in town).

Town government was among the last institutions to see Black faces. The first Black teachers in the town's public schools were not hired until the twenty-first century, almost 100 years later than the first Black student graduated from Phillipsburg High School. In 2015 Bianca Flowers was appointed to the board of the Phillipsburg Housing Authority. She was the first African-American to serve the town on any board. In 2016

Mrs. Vickie Mendes-Branch was elected to the Phillipsburg Board of Education with the second highest vote tally ever recorded for a school board candidate.

Vickie Mendes-Branch

That year was also notable for the election of Ms. Gayle Rogers as the president of the Friends of the Phillipsburg Free Public Library. In 2017, Lee Clark won a contested primary to become a Democratic Party candidate for Phillipsburg town council, but failed to win in the general election. On February 1, 2019, he was appointed to the board of Phillipsburg Housing Authority. He resigned on September 1, 2019 to accept an appointment to town council. He failed to win election to a full term in November. However, on the same day, Mrs. Mendes-Branch was reelected to a second term on the school board. Two years later in November 2021, Lee Clark was elected with the most votes of the six candidates vying for the three available seats on town council.

The integration of Black residents to the educational, religious and government institutions gained momentum starting with the Great Depression and maintained a slow boil in the Phillipsburg area. It wasn't until the twenty-first century that Black residents received regular positions of authority in the region.

Chapter 4

Biographies of notable Black individuals and families

In the first three chapters of this book, readers may have noticed some familiar names as they pop up in repeated instances of Phillipsburg history. In this chapter, readers will learn the more about these families.

DeMott Family

The best documented Black family in nineteenth century Phillipsburg is Thomas DeMott, as Easton's newspapers and churches chronicled the family's events. Among the free Blacks identified in the 1830 census in Greenwich Township was a man named Thomas Demut. He was head of his own household, between 36 and 55 years old and living with a woman between 24 and 35 years old and a boy younger than ten in the house. On April 28, 1837 Thomas DeMott purchased property in Phillipsburg along the New Jersey Turnpike (now called Main Street) from Peter Skillman for the sum of $500.00, making him the first known non-European property owner in Phillipsburg. He or his descendants were counted in every Phillipsburg census through 1890. He and his wife Jane raised two children, Henry and Ann, while Mr. DeMott worked as a hostler. The 1850 and 1860 censuses reveal that Thomas DeMott, his wife and children could read and write. The values given for his real ($1500 in 1860) and personal property ($300 in 1860) show he was, almost certainly, one of the wealthiest Black residents of Warren County.

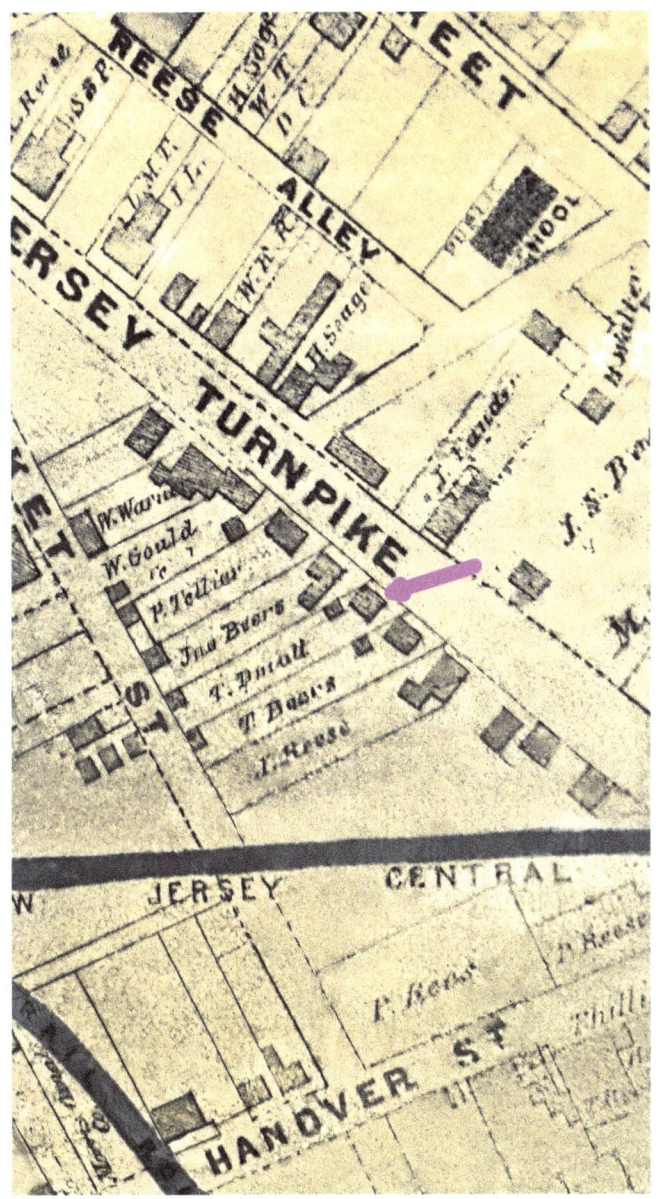

1857 map in Marx room of Easton Area Public Library
showing location of DeMott home

29

1874 map showing DeMott home on Randall St[36]

On December 15, 1863 he sold his prime real estate to the Morris & Essex Railroad for $1800--a considerable profit. The track was laid directly through the location of Mr. DeMott's house. A week after the sale, he purchased another property on Randall Street from Henry Segreaves for $700. Mr. DeMott's obituary reported that he died tragically in an accident when he was struck by a Morris & Essex train as he gathered coal along its tracks on September 20, 1872. The minister of Easton's First Presbyterian performed the funeral.[37]

---

[36] Beers, F. W. *County Atlas of Warren New Jersey,* 1874, p.47
[37] First Presbyterian Church records, September 21, 1872

The DeMotts were active participants in First Presbyterian Church in Easton. Thomas' wife and daughter were both baptized there. On June 29, 1863 his daughter was married to James Spruell by First Presbyterian's minister. When that same son-in-law James Spruell was arrested in 1869, he had legal representation. (Mr. Spruell's story is presented in great detail in Chapter 5).

In 1879 Ann DeMott Spruell married Isaac Smalley of Victoria, Vancouver Island. The notice of her second marriage was published in the Easton Express.[38] Thomas DeMott's grandson James K. Spruell was living with his grandmother Jane and working as a janitor in the Phillipsburg municipal building in 1890. After leaving for employment in a shore resort, James K. Spruell contracted malaria and died in 1893 at the age of 24. His obituary noted that he had been separated for some time from the unnamed white woman whom he had married.[39]

Some Early Shared Surnames

Three persons with the Duncan surname appear in some of Warren County's earliest records. Euphemia (Effie) Dunken married Robert Miller in 1830 and then Martin Freeman in 1844. Joseph Dunkon and his family appear in the 1840 census. Thomas Duncan married Eunice Osmun in 1841. There is no evidence to determine if their common name indicated a blood relationship or if they might have shared a common owner. Meanwhile, the Mingo surname of Betty Mingo Firman (manumitted in Oxford Township in 1818) and Catherine Mingo Duncan may have African origin or indicate descent from the Mingo group of Iroquoian Indians.

---

[38] *Easton Express*, February 28, 1879
[39] *Easton Daily Free Press*. August 7, 1893

Joseph Duncan family

Joseph and Catherine (Mingo) Duncan appear in Greenwich in the 1840 census with their two children under the age of ten. By the 1860 census, they are officially in Phillipsburg proper, where Joseph was a hostler for William Hartpence's hotel. Joseph and Catherine were two of the founding members of the First Colored Lutheran Church in Easton. Joseph was elected the first deacon for the congregation. By 1880, Joseph and Catherine disappear from the census records

Still living in town in 1880 were Joseph's youngest son, George, then married to Henrietta, and Joseph's oldest daughter, Christianna, married to Mahlon Chamberlain. The Chamberlin family will be explored as a separate surname later in this chapter.

Joseph Duncan's oldest son, Francis, had married in 1858 and lived in town with his wife, the former Rachel Freeman, and daughter, Alice. Francis enlisted at Easton in Company E of the 24th Regiment, United States Colored Troops under the name Frank Dunkins. His unit guarded rebel prisoners of war at Point Lookout, Md., and then were tasked with preserving order in the six counties surrounding Roanoke, Va.

After his discharge in October 1865, Francis settled in Maryland. The outcome of his first marriage is unknown. However, in 1893, he married a Maryland woman named Josephine. They moved to Burlington County, NJ and raised a daughter, Anne Marie, there. By 1915 he had returned to the Phillipsburg area. Frank lived in Alpha, NJ until shortly before his death at Burlingame, NJ in 1920. Frank was buried in the Baptist cemetery in Burlington, NJ.

Thomas Duncan family

Thomas Duncan grew up in Greenwich Township and was attending school in 1850. He was definitely a resident of Phillipsburg when he married Sophia More of Easton in Christ Lutheran Church in 1863.

Thomas enlisted on December 11, 1863 and served in Co B of the 22nd Regiment of the United States Colored Troops. He was part of a detachment sent to protect workers digging a canal at Dutch Gap on the James River. Its completion would have allowed Union forces to avoid Confederate artillery. He rejoined his unit to participate in the attacks on Petersburg and Richmond, Va., and to march in President Lincoln's funeral procession. They were then sent to pacify Texas and to patrol the Rio Grande border after the French installed Emperor Maximillian in Mexico.

Thomas mustered out on October 18, 1865 at Brownsville, Texas. In his absence Sophia had suffered an untimely death in 1864. After the war, Thomas married Charlotte Freeman in Christ Church, Easton, and moved to Alexandria Township in Hunterdon County, NJ. He later purchased a home in Pohatcong Township. Thomas died between 1915 and 1920.

His son, Spencer, would return to Phillipsburg by 1895. Spencer married Carolinda Folks of Virginia in 1896 and they begab to raise a family in town. When Spencer died of pneumonia in Easton Hospital in 1906, he left a widow and five small children.

22 U.S.C.T.

Thomas Duncan

............, *Co. K*, 22 Reg't U. S. Col'd Inf.

Appears on

Company Descriptive Book

of the organization named above.

DESCRIPTION.

Age *24* years; height *5* feet *7* inches.

Complexion *blk*

Eyes *blk*; hair *blk*

Where born *Phillipsburg, N. J.*

Occupation *Farmer*

ENLISTMENT. *mus. in*

When *Dec 11*, 186*3*

Where *Phila. Pa.*

By whom *Col Wagner* term *3* y'rs.

mus. in by Lt Burke.

Remarks: *In action at Petersburg June 15/64, Dutch Gap Aug 16/64.*

Thomas Duncan Service Record

34

Mahlon Chamberlin family

Mahlon Chamberlin and his wife Christianna Duncan had at least seven children. Their daughters married John Lyle (Catharine), Walter Lee (Agnes), Charles Ross (Sarah) and Edward Wilson (Mary Ellen) and raised families locally. Granddaughter Sadie Wilson was married in 1894 to Augustus A'Vant, a story for another paragraph.

Their only son George had the misfortune of being arrested when his companion James Spruell was accused of murder in a deadly altercation with a gang of white residents. The subsequent roundup of most of Phillipsburg's Black men likely influenced George's decision to move south to Virginia after the matter was resolved.

Mahlon registered for the Civil War draft, but did not serve. In 1881, eleven years after the first Black residents voted in Phillipsburg, Mahlon was nominated as the Republican candidate for Pound Keeper in the town's first ward. Despite only seven Black men of voting age in the ward, Mahlon received 145 votes.[40] His opponent James Connelly, however, gathered 151 votes and was elected. Had Mahlon not been deathly ill during the final week of the campaign, he might have been, not only the first Black candidate, but the first Black person to win an election in Phillipsburg. Sadly, he died of pneumonia the day after the election. Mahlon's obituary remembered him as a man who was "too heavy for light work and too light for heavy work."[41] and lauded "Mahl" as a landmark: someone with many excellent traits who would be missed. He was buried in Easton Cemetery, as would be his wife Christianna and three of their daughters Agnes Lee, Katie Lyle and Sarah Ross and their families.

---

[40]   *Evening Free Press*, April 12, 1881
[41]   *Easton Daily Express*, April 13, 1881, p. 3

Ward Clerk
Hiram Meyers, Rep.......................................146
J. H. Brensinger, Cit...................................160
                                                        ___
Brensinger's maj....................................... 14
Pound Keeper.
Jacob Beigle...   5
Mahlon Chamberlain.....................................145
James Connelly, Cit....................................151
                                                        ___
Connelly over Chamberlain..............................   6
Justice of the Peace.
D. McConnell, Dem......................................107
J. W. Low, Rep...145
                                                        ___
Low's maj.. 38

Results from election on April 11, 1881 in Ward 1, Phillipsburg[42]

Innes Families

Charles and Martha Innes with son Joseph were living in
Phillipsburg in 1860, while John and his family lived near St.
James' Lutheran church in Greenwich Township, NJ. John's
mother was an unnamed slave owned by Robert Innes, Sr.,
whose surname John took. John's labors on behalf of the
church earned him an extended tribute in an Easton
newspaper.

> There resides at St. James Ev. Lutheran Church,
> Greenwich, Warren County, a colored man named
> John Innes, who has held the position of sexton in the
> above named church for a period of thirty-one years
> on the 1st of April last. His history is an interesting
> one, and is deserving of more than a passing notice. At
> the age of four years he was bound out by his mother

---

[42] "The Election" *The Daily Free Press*, April 12, 1881

to a Major Hougabout, who lived near St. James' Church until he should reach the age of twenty-one years. He not only remained until the close of the time for which he was indentured, but continued with his old master for three years longer. He then spent six months in the village of Bloomsbury, where he was married. On the 1st of April following his marriage, he removed with his wife to the vicinity of the church where he was raised, and has served in the capacity of Sexton ever since. During that time he has dug over six hundred graves, except four or five graves, which were moved by others, he has opened every grave in the burying ground of St. James' since his entrance upon his duty as sexton. It is also worthy of notice that the church was opened by himself for thirty-one years, except on four occasions on account of sickness or absence. He has enjoyed the confidence and esteem of the congregation, and is highly respected by all. In the long period during which he has served the church, nothing even of the most trifling character has occurred to mar the pleasure between him and his employers, and should his life be spared, may many more years be added to the already long term of his service.

It is doubtful if another case like the above can be produced. Usually the term of service is not of long continuance, because of difference between him and the church he serves, or on account of an unwillingness to remain long in such a position, but the case of J. Innes, of St. James' church, proves that sometimes a difficult duty may be performed for a long time to the satisfaction of all concerned.[43]

---

[43] *Evening Free Press*, April 27, 1871

Nelson Truax

Nelson Truax was born in Burlington County about 1835. By 1860, he was living in Phillipsburg and employed as a hostler in William Hartpence's hotel. He enlisted in the United States Colored Troops on February 16, 1865 in Easton. Assigned to Company D of the 24th Regiment, he was promoted to Sergeant. Before his unit left Camp William Penn, the first and largest Federal training facility for African-American soldiers, they were addressed by Harriet Tubman. After a month and a half guarding Confederate prisoners at Point Lookout, Md., Nelson and his regiment were sent to the Richmond, Va. region in July 1865. They spent about seven weeks near Roanoke preserving order while the government distributed supplies to the needy. Nelson was discharged on October 10 and returned to Phillipsburg. He was baptized in December 1865 at the First Colored Lutheran Church in Easton. By 1870, he had married Adeline and returned to South Jersey. They raised their family in Cinnaminson and Delran, while Nelson labored in area farms. He died on October 19, 1909 and was buried in Beverly National Cemetery, Beverly, NJ.

Augustus A'Vant family

Augustus A'Vant was born in North Carolina in 1854, the son of Augustus and Elizabeth (Bradley) A'Vant. He earned a degree from Howard University in Washington, DC, and was qualified as a public school teacher. Unable to get a position in his field, he moved to Phillipsburg and worked at the pipe foundry on Sitgreaves Street. On September 11, 1894, he married Sadie Wilson, a fourth-generation town resident, in the First Methodist Church, Phillipsburg. Augustus was "one of the most prominent citizens"E[44] in the town's Black community and a leader in the Twilight Social Club and Colored Odd Fellows. After his untimely death in 1908 and burial in Phillipsburg Cemetery, his pregnant widow, six surviving children, and mother-in-law, Mary Wilson, moved to

---

[44]   *Easton Free Press,* September 29, 1908, p. 1

Providence, RI. Sadie remarried to Walter Abrams and the
family remained in Rhode Island permanently.

Augustus A'Vant

Beidleman family

John and Hetty Beidleman raised eight children in the Huntington neighborhood (just south of Phillipsburg and part of the old Beidleman estate). Their sons Hezekiah and Alexander were working in the New Jersey towns of Roxbury and Mendham when the Civil War began. In a double wedding on January 1, 1862, Hezekiah married Charlotte Ray, while his brother married Margaret Jane Ballentine. Both young men enlisted in the United States Navy in 1863.

ENLISTMENTS AT NEW YORK IN 1863.

Enlistment of Alexander Beidleman

They were landsmen and coal heavers on board the USS Ottawa. Their ship participated in the blockade of the Georgia and South Carolina seaports during 1864. After the war, Alexander settled and raised his family in Morris Township, Morris County. Hezekiah went to Morristown at first, then moved to Newark, NJ, Long Branch, NJ, and also Manhattan in New York City. Both men received Navy pensions. Alexander died in 1911 and is buried in Evergreen Cemetery in Morristown. Hezekiah died in 1925 in Mineola, NY.

Daniel Prime

Daniel Prime was born in Easton on March 26, 1843, the son of Samuel and Rachel (Anderson). He moved to Phillipsburg and worked as a barber before enlisting in the Massachusetts Infantry on May 13, 1863. A member of Company H, 54th Regiment, Daniel took part in the assault on Confederate held Fort Wagner, which protected Charleston harbor, just two months after his enlistment. His service was distinguished by caring for a wounded soldier from his company. Daniel removed his blouse and wrapped it around his comrade to stop the bleeding, then carried the man away from the field of battle. The bravery of Daniel and his fellow soldiers was a catalyst for the organization of the United States Colored Troops which enlisted about 180,000 Black men to fight for the Union. Daniel's unit saw further action in Florida, particularly in protecting the retreat of white Union troops after their defeat in the battle of Olustee. After the war, Daniel returned home, married Angeline Jefferson (from Roxbury, N.J.) and raised his family in Easton. He was employed by Charles Meeker in his stove store and tinsmithing operations. In addition, Daniel was an exceptional cook, who found employment at Harry Seip's Cafe and other restaurants. His skills were in high demand for clambakes and other banquets. Daniel was an honorary member of Easton's Humane Fire Company, No. 1 and was elected a member of the New Jersey Exempt Firemen's Association in gratitude for his services to the Hoboken chapter of that organization. Upon his death in 1931, he was buried in Easton Heights Cemetery.

Abraham James family

Abraham James married Catherine Case on May 14, 1831 in St. John's Lutheran Church, Easton. On April 3, 1840, they moved to the Greenwich Township property he inherited in the will of the Rev. William B. Sloan, pastor of Greenwich Presbyterian Church.

Their son Alfred James was a waiter until he enlisted at Philadelphia on January 4, 1863. He served in Company K, 22 Inf Regiment of the US Colored Troops. On detached service with the sharpshooter division, he was wounded in action in the battle for Petersburg, Va. on September 29, 1864, and died in the army hospital at Point of Rocks, Va. on October 11. He was buried in City Point National Cemetery in Hopewell, Va., and a pension was sent to his father.

| 22 | U. S. C. T. |

Alfred James

........................., Co. _K_ , 22 Reg't U. S. Col'd Inf.

Appears on

Company Descriptive Book

of the organization named above.

DESCRIPTION.

Age _35_ years; height _5_ feet _4 3/4_ inches.

Complexion _Black_

Eyes _Black_ ; hair _Black_

Where born _Phillips New Jersey_
N. Hampton

Occupation _Waiter_

ENLISTMENT.

When _Jan. 4_ , 186_4_.

Where _Philada, Pa._

By whom _Col Wagner_ ; term _3_ y'rs.

Remarks _Detached as member_
of Div. Sharpshooters
June 27" 1864. Wounded
in action near New
Market road Henrico Co.
Va. Sept 29" 1864 Died of
wounds at 18th Army
Corps Hospital Point of
Rocks, Va. Oct. 11th 1864.

Another of Abraham's sons, William James, registered for the Civil War draft, but did not serve. One of Abraham's daughters, Elizabeth, married Abraham Furman, while daughter Anna James married James Furman. Abraham James moved away to Newark where he worked as a stableman until his death in 1892.

Nathan Hackett family

One Phillipsburg resident who arrived in town later in life was Nathaniel (Nathan) W. Hackett. He was born in 1841 to Thomas and Frances Hackett in Bethlehem Township, Hunterdon County.

Nathan enlisted as a soldier during the Civil War and served in Company C, 45th Regiment in the US Colored Troops. After his discharge he enlisted in the US Navy in 1864. He received a naval pension for his service. After the war he returned to Bethlehem Township where he married Lydia Blakens in 1870 and worked on the railroad. His son William married and moved to Phillipsburg before 1900 to work at a cement mill.

Nathan's daughter Mary married Daniel Freeman who began working at the pipe foundry in Phillipsburg. Nathan and Lydia left Hunterdon County and moved to Phillipsburg to live with Mary and Daniel by 1905. Nathan died on February 17, 1920 and is buried in the Civil War veterans' section of Phillipsburg Cemetery.

James Miller

James Miller was living and working on Jacob Hulshizer's farm in Greenwich township in 1850. By 1860 he had married Ruth Ann Lawson, a native of New Brunswick, NJ. On December 11, 1863, he went to Philadelphia along with Thomas Duncan where he enlisted in the United States Colored Troops and was also assigned to Company B, of the 22nd Regiment. Along with Thomas Duncan, he spent time on detached service at Dutch Gap and was discharged in Brownsville, Texas after service on the Mexican border in December 1865. While James disappeared from the records after his discharge, his wife Ruth was an active participant in the First Colored Church of Easton until her death in 1893. Ruth was buried in Easton Cemetery.

22 **U.S.C.T.**

James Miller

Pvt., Co. B, 22 Reg't U. S. Col'd Infantry.

Appears on

Company Muster Roll

for *July & Aug* , 186*4*.

Present or absent *Absent*

Stoppage, $ ..... 100 for ....

Due Gov't, $ ..... 100 for ....

Remarks: *On detached service at Dutch Gap since Aug. 2, 1864 Due on or before April 19/61*

Service record of James Miller

Joseph Hortman

Joseph B. Hortman, son of Andrew and Ann, was born in 1865 in Franklin Township, Warren County. Joseph married Alice Thorpe, a Virginia native, in 1887. They raised three children: Mamie (who married Edward Prime), Myrtle (who married Clawell White) and Sophie.

Joseph came to Brainard Street in Phillipsburg about 1896 during the twenty years he was employed as a dining car waiter for the Lehigh Valley Railroad. He then switched to the Delaware, Lackawanna & Western railroad. In his last years Joseph was a steward at the Elks Club in town. Alice was a member of the African Methodist Episcopal Church in Easton. Joseph died in 1922, as did Alice, three years later. They were buried in Phillipsburg's Fairmount Cemetery.

William Furman family

The Furman family has deep, documented roots in the area. On September 17, 1818 the Rev. Garner A. Hunt in Oxford Township, N.J. granted Betty Mingo Firman her freedom through a writ of manumission. In the 1830 and 1840 federal censuses William Furman and his family were recorded in the township. Born in 1796, William's wife Phebe was the daughter of an Englishman Peter Young and a slave named Dina. Phebe's birth and death were recorded in the family Bible of Thomas Kennedy.[45]

 At the age of 27, Phebe was granted freedom by Thomas Kennedy in 1824 in Greenwich. Her daughter Sarah Furman married Henry Prime at Easton's St. John's Lutheran Church in 1849. In 1850 and 1860, Phebe Furman, with her four children, was living in Greenwich as the owner of real estate worth $200. Her property on South Main Street in Stewartsville was next door to that of Robert S. Kennedy, son of her former owner, Thomas.

---

[45]   Kennedy Family Bible, Appendix A

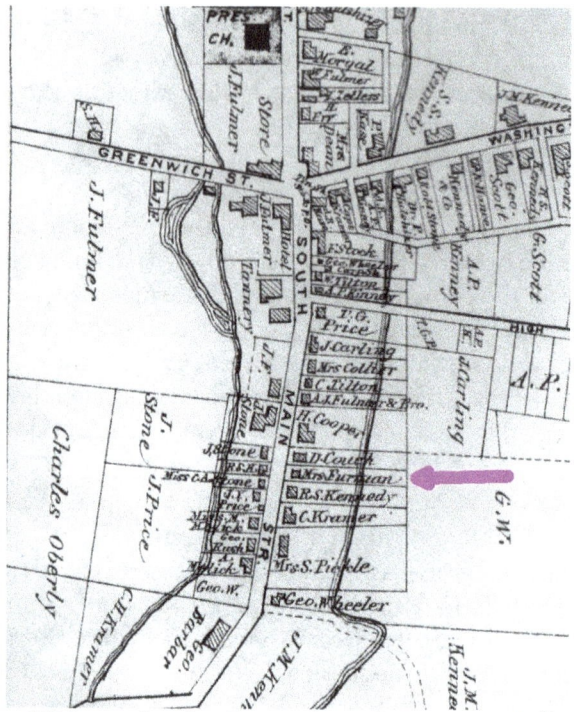

1874 map showing Furman home in Stewartsville[46]

Phebe's son James Furman married Anna James in 1861. They caused quite a stir in Stewartsville and in the Easton news when Anna gave birth to twins in 1870.[47]

Phebe's son Abraham married Elizabeth James in 1862. He worked as a teamster in Newark, NJ for a time, then returned to Stewartsville. Phebe died in 1885, aged 89 years.

[46] Beers, F. W. *County Atlas of Warren New Jersey,* 1874, p.43
[47] *Easton Express,* July 7, 1870, p. 3.

Henry Wells

In 1868, Henry Wells became the second Black property owner within the Phillipsburg town limits when he came from Roxbury in Morris county to purchase property on Rose Street from Joseph Howell. Henry settled into his home with his wife Susanna (Williams) and four children: Henrietta, George, Charles and William. According to the census records eight year old George was a student in town, but his school was not identified. Unfortunately, Henry was unable to keep that house. With his mortgage in arrears, Henry saw his home sold at a sheriff's sale in 1874 to John H. Hagerty. By 1880 Henry was a widower in Easton where he died in 1895. His son Charles married and moved to Newark. Son William worked as a waiter in Trenton and Philadelphia. His daughter married Charles Holmes in 1871.

The Burr/Outen families

Andrew Burr and his wife Dianna (Furman) raised their family in Lows Hollow, near Stewartsville, N.J. Their daughter Anna Augusta, born 1855, married James B. Hogan in Stewartsville Lutheran Church on December 29, 1879. By 1885, the Hogans were living in Phillipsburg, where James worked as a teamster. By 1900, James was working as a dining car cook and the family had moved to Easton. Although their daughter Anna, who married George Craig, was the only one of the seven Hogan children to reach adulthood, Anna Craig was only 38 when she died in 1918. Anna Burr Hogan died in Easton Hospital in 1927 and was buried in Easton Cemetery.

Andrew's son, Charles Burr, born about 1860, married Mary Elizabeth Fox in 1885 at St. Luke's Episcopal Church, the earliest known marriage of a Black couple in a Phillipsburg church. Charles then raised his family in Harmony.

Andrew's second son, Arthur Valentine Burr, born in 1868, was initially employed as a porter. Arthur married Mary E. Outen (born in Richmond, Va. to James Outen and the former

Mary Johnson) before 1895 and lived on Sitgreaves St. in Phillipsburg. By 1905, the couple had moved to a house on Howard St. where they lived the rest of their lives. Arthur Burr left the railroad and became a stationary engineer at Tippet & Wood Boiler Works (a job he would keep for more than 30 years). Mary Outen Burr died in 1950 while her husband Arthur died in 1955.

By 1895, Mary Outen Burr's sister, Martha was a live-in employee of the J. T. Blair family in Phillipsburg. Martha soon married Frank Smith, a dining car steward. They set up house on Cross Street, beside the A'vant, Hackett, and Duncan families. Frank progressed to a position as a mail clerk on the railroad and they moved to Bethlehem, Pa. Martha later moved to Easton.

Cornelius Outen, younger brother of Mary Outen Burr, was living with Arthur and Mary in 1900 and working at the boiler works. By 1905 Cornelius, his wife Martha, and their daughters Lydia and Ellen were living on Cross St. The entire family disappear from available records after 1905.

Shortly after 1900, Mary Outen Burr's sister Lillian arrived in the area. Lillian married Pohatcong native George Freeman, who was a teamster at the boiler works. Lillian stayed in Phillipsburg until her death in 1950.

A third of Mary's sisters, Anna Verna Outen, took a circuitous route from Virginia to Phillipsburg. She first traveled to Leominster, Mass., where she married Charles Monroe on June 8, 1901. Anna, Charles and their four children moved to Phillipsburg in 1910, next door to Arthur and Mary on Howard St. Charles swiftly found employment at the boiler works. Charles and family quickly returned to Massachusetts where a fifth child was born in 1912. However, Verna then moved to New York State, first to Mount Vernon and then to the Bronx. Verna and Charles both died after 1940.

Harry Case

A resident of Pohatcong Township, Harry Case Jr, was the first Black student known to graduate from Phillipsburg High School. Born on February 25, 1909 in New Hope, PA, he grew up near his grandparents Harry and Caroline (Freeman) Martin in Warren Glen, a neighborhood in Pohatcong Township. He was the son of Harry and Margaret May (Martin) Case. His great-grandfather James Martin and great--great-grandfather Hector Martin had been residents of Alexandria Township, Hunterdon County, just across the Musconetcong River from Warren Glen. Harry graduated in 1929 with the caption "surmounting all obstacles" beneath his yearbook photo. He played varsity baseball for two years so skillfully that the class poem devoted an entire stanza to his prowess on the diamond:

> When Harry Case steps up to bat
> It's a hit without doubt
> Because he's not like the Casey of old
> He's never yet struck out."[48]

After graduating from Phillipsburg High School, Harry worked at Riegel Paper mill, just as his father and grandfather had done. Harry married Helen White from Washington, NJ and they had a son Roger. Harry later married Mary Johnson. Harry was a member of Greenwich Presbyterian Church, Masonic Temple Absalom Jones, and the Blue Mountain Radio Club. Harry was captain of the Pohatcong Civil Defense Corps. Harry died on November 30,1977 in Phillipsburg and was buried in Greenwich Cemetery.

---

[48] *Phillipsburg High School Yearbook,* 1929

Harry Case, Jr

The Phillipsburg High School graduation of Harry's son, Roger Lamont Case, in 1958 made them the first Black family with two generations of graduates wearing the garnet and gray. Roger inherited some of his father's athletic talent and excelled on the track. Roger married Martha Tyndall and worked at Ingersoll-Rand. Roger was a member of the New Jersey National Guard, The Reliance Hose Company and Easton Lodge, F&AM. Roger died at the age of 37, leaving behind his widow and a son Robert.

Esau Wallace family

The family of Esau and Rebecca Wallace was one of the first Black families to settle in Phillipsburg after World War I. Their oldest daughters, Rose and Ruth, were born in South Carolina in 1921 and 1922, respectively, while daughter Anna was born in Phillipsburg in 1927. Esau Wallace worked for the telephone company and in road construction before landing a job at Bethlehem Steel. Ruth Wallace married Edward Fox and died in Philadelphia in 1966.

Easu was perhaps best known as an evangelist, who spoke throughout the Lehigh Valley while serving as an assistant pastor at the First Baptist Church in Anderson, N.J. After his wife Rebecca died in 1934, Esau married Ella Davis. Esau died in Easton in 1990 at the age of 98.

In 1946, Anna Wallace was the first resident of the town to graduate from Phillipsburg High School. Known for a laugh that was "out of this world,"[49] Anna reportedly could not stop singing in the halls and in Glee Club. Anna married a Mr. Young and lived in Philadelphia. She died before her father.

Carl Martin family

In 1933, Phillipsburg High School saw its second Black graduate, another resident of Pohatcong Township. Born to Carl and Emma Martin, Elizabeth (Betty) Laura Martin was a first cousin to Harry Case Jr. Betty took part in the Book and Mask Club and its dramatic productions. Her yearbook description "studious and bright"[50] was certainly accurate. She went on to earn bachelor's and master's degrees. She devoted a lifetime of service to public health, institutional, private duty

[49]   *Phillipsburg High School Yearbook*, 1946
[50]   *Phillipsburg High School Yearbook*, 1933

and school nursing. Close to her heart was her time as a school nurse at Cinnaminson, NJ Middle School.

Betty married Dr. Ralph Rudolph Tolver, a veteran of World War II, who had served as a major in a medical battalion of the Army's 92nd Infantry Division. They raised three children. Betty died in 2012 at the age of 95. Betty and Ralph are buried in Beverly National Cemetery in Burlington County, NJ.

Betty's brother, James R. Martin, maintained the family scholastic tradition and graduated from Phillipsburg High School in 1934, a year after his sister. A star on the track, he set the school record in the 100-yard dash and was also part of the record setting relay team. Off the field he shared some of his other talents onstage in the school play, the operetta and the Glee Club. He joined the US Navy and served during World War II.

Carolyn Martin
Carolyn Alberta Martin followed the examples of her cousins--James Martin, Betty Martin and Harry Case Jr. by graduating from Phillipsburg High School in 1939. She sang with the Glee Club and was a member of the Girl Reserves. In the class prophecy, her classmates predicted that she would become a nurse (like her cousin Betty) and work at a brand new hospital they hoped would be built in Phillipsburg.

In her youngest years, Carolyn lived with her parents, James and Anna Broadhead Martin, on Sitgreaves Street while her father worked at the pipe foundry. They later moved to Warren Glen and her father joined the workforce of the paper mill alongside his father, Harry, and brother Carl. Carolyn married Sidney James Groves in 1942 and moved to Washington, NJ, where she was active in the Mt. Pisgah African Methodist Episcopal Church. After dying there in 1996, Carolyn was buried in Greenwich Cemetery.

Martin Freeman family

In 1840, Martin Freeman, son of Isaac and Lizzie, had a family with three children under the age of ten in Alexandria Township. In 1844, he married Euphemia (Duncan) Miller and they moved to Greenwich Township.

On November 8, 1858, Martin purchased land in Greenwich Township (later Pohatcong Township) on a ridge above Warren Glen from John and Charity Sinclair for 90 dollars. Martin Freeman married Harriet Martin in 1860.

His numerous descendants intermarried with the local Duncan, Furman, Martin, James, and Hackett families, as well as people who arrived from other states. Martin Sr. did some farming on his own land and made dandelion wine.

In later years he worked for the paper mill. "He was not allowed to work inside the plant. Blacks were restricted to grounds maintenance, teamster work, operation of the filtering plant, and the like."[51]

His son, Martin Jr., was employed for more than 50 years by Warren Manufacturing. He transported information, personnel, mail and supplies between Riegelsville and Warren Glen. On weekends Martin Jr. operated a stagecoach from the Warren Glen to town on Saturday nights and to church on Sunday mornings.

The historical record is unclear whether Martin Freeman, Sr. or his son, Martin Jr., was the fiddler who performed for dances of the Black community's social club in Pohatcong Township. At various times some Freemans have lived in Phillipsburg itself. Martin Freeman Sr. died on July 17, 1893.

---

[51]   *Pohatcong: The Prologue*, p. 64

Cleveland Wooten

Born in Helena, Ga. in 1899, PFC Cleveland "Bam" Wooten served in France in Company A, 314th Service Battalion during World War I.

By 1930, he had moved to Somerville, NJ where he worked in road construction. By 1937, he had married Myrtle McIntosh and had moved to Phillipsburg, where he worked for the Works Progress Administration. He was then employed by Alpha Portland Cement as a dinky operator. He was a charter member and trustee of Grace Baptist Church.

Myrtle worked 25 years as a domestic employee in the household of Richard Weldon in Carpentersville, NJ.. Myrtle died in Allentown, Pa. in 1974 and Cleveland died in 1976 in the veterans hospital in Dublin, Ga. They were buried in Northampton Memorial Shrine, Plamer Township, Pa.

Charles Utley

During his time at Phillipsburg High School, Charles "Bucky" Utley was elected president of the class of 1969. He excelled as a running back for the football team and was a key player for the school's basketball and baseball teams After attending Robert Morris and Duquesne universities, Charles chose to stay in the Pittsburgh area and became an insurance agent. He died in Monroeville, Pa. on July 10, 2022.

Officers of PHS class of 1969
Seated: Charles Utley, Diane Hagaman, Michael Emrick
Standing: Geoffrey Hanisak, Mr. Buralli, Mr. Hughes

Chapter 5

Two Homicides, Different Outcomes

The contrasting accounts of two homicides and the treatment of the accused, separated by 76 years, provide a unique look at the Black encounters with the local justice system. In the more modern case, Mr. James Spruell's legal representation and access to witnesses for the defense were undoubtedly factors in the variation in sentencing. For more on his wife's family, see the biography of Thomas DeMott in Chapter Four.

1795

Robert Waldren (aka Mulatto Bob) was a slave, the property of the Stewart family of Greenwich Township. By reputation, he maintained an excellent character. His life took a tragic turn in the spring of 1795 as recounted by this Easton newspaper 1833:

> On Easter Monday last, thirty-eight years ago, a number of negroes came over in the flat from Jersey to the Hollow, now dignified with the cognomen of Delaware Ward. They came to a wedding and a row. They assembled before old Squire Able's about ten o'clock at night, when and where a set battle was fought between Mulatto Bob and Negro David. The fight soon became general, and the whole troop of negroes inspired by fun and rum, engaged in the manual of the fist. . . About ten minutes after the affray, Mulatto Bob armed himself with an axe from a neighboring wood pile, attacked Negro David, who defended himself with a setting pole, and in the struggle occasioned by the attempt of the negroes to disarm him, he struck David on the head and knockedhim down. While attempting to rise, he struck him again, with the sharp edge, which penetrated the head to the eyes, until the brains covered the axe. The

whole posse of the negroes, excepting two, immediately fled to the forks of the Delaware, now called the point, and loosening the bateaux and all other small craft along the shore, transported themselves with the greatest expedition across to Jersey. David languished three days with his brain thus split open, and died. Mulatto Bob was arrested in Jersey and delivered by the constable of Greenwich to the Sheriff of Northampton on the Delaware. He was shortly after indicted and tried for the murder of Negro David, before Chief Justice McKean, and convicted and sentenced to be hung. Sheriff Craig swung the poor fellow from off a cart on "Gallows Hill," a hill which received its name from the fate of Mulatto Bob. . . That spot will be remembered in history and tradition, as the spot where was atoned the only murder in old Northampton for half a century.

In consequence of the inadmissibility of the only witness who could have exculpated Bob (the witness being a slave and therefore not permitted to testify) and also in consequence of his previous good character, many respectable citizens of Sussex (now Warren), New Jersey petitioned the executive for his pardon. Bob was brought up by the Stewart family in Greenwich, and had always maintained an excellent character. David was the property of Garret Striker of the same place, and in the language of one of the witnesses, was "a worthless daog," The body of Bob was delivered to his Jersey friends, who took it across the river and used some exertion to resuscitate it. The veins bled freely, but the vital spark had fled forever.[52]

Robert was convicted at a Court of Oyer and Terminer in Easton on June 22, 1795. Despite the petitions for pardon,

---

[52] *Evening Free Press*, July 20, 1871 Although the original 1833 newspaper did not survive, the story was reprinted in 1871.

Governor Thomas Mifflin issued the warrant for execution on September 22, 1795. Robert Waldren was hanged on Gallows Hill (near the present day intersection of Fifth and Washington streets) in Easton on October 24, 1795.[53]

1869

James Spruell was just one of the Black persons, born in Southern states, who spent some time in Phillipsburg in the 1800's. After his escape from slavery in North Carolina, James eventually arrived in Phillipsburg. His stay in town was brief, as was typical, but that time was eventful for him and the town.

On June 29, 1863, James married Anna Jane DeMott, the daughter of Phillipsburg's first Black homeowner. They had four children: Edward (1863-1869), Jenny Ann (1865-1866), James K. (1867-1893) and Emory (1870-1871). Edward was buried in the churchyard of the First Presbyterian Church of Easton. It is likely that Jenny and Emory were buried there, as well.

James enlisted in the United States Colored Troops on February 16, 1865 in Easton. Along with Nelson Truax (see his biography in Chapter Four), James was assigned to Company D of the 24th Regiment. Before his unit left Camp William Penn, the first and largest Federal training facility for African-American soldiers, they were addressed by Harriet Tubman.

After a month and a half guarding Confederate prisoners at Point Lookout, Md., the regiment was sent to the region of Richmond, Va. in July 1865. They spent about seven weeks near Roanoke preserving order while the government

---

[53]   *Pennsylvania Archives, Ninth Series*, vol. 2, p.1019

distributed supplies to the needy. On October 1, 1865, James was mustered out of service.

The Event

On October 5, 1869, James Spruell and some friends attended a meeting of the Colored Drum Corps in Easton. As they crossed the bridge back into Phillipsburg, they were accosted by some white men.

Mr. Spruell shot and killed William Nightingale after being attacked by the "victim." Phillipsburg police officers Brown and Nightingale were ordered "to search all the residences of the negroes in town and arrest all the male inmates."[54] James Spruell, George Chamberlin and Charles Robinson were arrested. Following is James' statement to the authorities.

My name is James Sproull. I was a slave in North Carolina, having been owned by a man also named Sproull. Escaped during the war to Newbern, NC, and engaged myself as servant to Adjutant Edward S. Carrell, of the 9th New Jersey Volunteers. Upon the death of Adjutant Carrell came to Phillipsburg, NJ where I married Ann DeMott. Did not return in the 9th New Jersey, but enlisted in a colored regiment and served until the close of the war, when I came back to Phillipsburg and have been employed driving team for Mr. Walter. Last evening, in company with Charles Perry, Daniel Benjamin, Giles Hub, Samuel Johnson, Vandesberger, Alexander Moore, George Merritt, George Chamberlin and Charles Robinson, I came to Easton. Was not in the habit of carrying a revolver, but as I had forty-five dollars belonging to the Drum Corps, I remarked to my wife that I believed I would take it in case someone should attack me on the bridge. On returning from the meeting we were attacked at the end of the bridge by some white men, one of whom grabbed George Chamberlin. I saw the

---

[54]   *Washington Star*, October 9, 1869

men put their hands in their pockets and pull out some bottles. We started and ran, the men throwing bottles at us. I ran up Main Street and being struck in the back with a bottle. Turned around and said to Nightingale, 'You are coming, are you? I don't want to hurt you.' or words to that effect. I then pulled my pistol and fired three shots.[55]

Repercussions

The coroner's inquest in Phillipsburg determined the next morning that Mr. Spruell was guilty of either manslaughter or murder. During the inquest's deliberations, groups of people in town discussed the details and reached their own conclusions as to whether it was murder or self defense.

There were residents who voiced their belief that he had acted in a legitimate act of self defense and was guilty of no crime at all. This was especially true of those who knew the dead man's reputation. Two days after James' departure for the Trenton, NJ jail, one Easton newspaper opined:

Of all classes of people it may be said that Phillipsburg has one of the worst, and it is much regretted by the better portion of that growing place. Sproell justly shelved one, and if Mayor Dean had ordered the police with their pistols to shoot several more, instead of, by silence, giving sanction to their mob acts in attempting to kill three negroes while in irons and under escort of the sheriff, it would have been well for the town. The men were drunk, noisy, and disturbing the peace, yet Mayor Dean looked on with as much peace of mind, and with the same satisfaction as he gazed upon his own picture when displayed in Riegel's window some time past. So much tolerance has been shown the drunken rowdies that infest Phillipsburg that respectable people fear to

---

[55] "Homicide in Phillipsburg," *Evening Free Press*, Easton, PA October 6, 1869, pg 3

walk its streets by night, and the men themselves boast
that they rule the town[56]

Threats of lynching were made but no attempt was made to
carry them out. While James, George and Charles were in leg
irons at the Bel-Del Railroad depot and awaiting their train
ride to jail in Trenton, a fight broke out between friends of the
accused and some white men.[57] An attempt was made to attack
the prisoners and a Black man named Edward Johnson was
stabbed.

With the assistance of town police, the sheriff successfully
loaded the prisoners into a baggage car. They were confined in
the Mercer County, NJ jail until the new Warren County jail
was completed. The census on June 14, 1870 recorded James
Spruell and William Nightingale as residents of the Warren
county jail in Belvidere.

James was represented by legal counsel who negotiated a plea
bargain to manslaughter in 1870. He was sentenced to five
years at hard labor in state prison. That same day his victim's
brother, William Nightingale, was convicted of assault and
battery for his attack on Charles Robinson at the train station
and sentenced to one year in state prison.[58]

After James' sentence was pronounced, there was some
sentiment in town that it was unduly harsh. No record of his
time in the Trenton prison survives, but after his release,
James and Ann went their separate ways. Ann married Isaac
Smalley while James married Perdilla Sanderson. James and
Perdilla had four children in Trenton between 1873 and 1881.
James Spruell died in Trenton on July 1, 1889 at the age of 49.

---

[56] "A Phillipsburg Mob," *Evening Free Press*, Easton, PA October
8, 1869
[57] "Murder in Phillipsburg," *Washington Star*, Washington, NJ
October 9, 1869
[58] *Evening Free Press*, September 29, 1870, p. 3

Afterword

The history of Black people in and around Phillipsburg has included a mixture of triumph and pain. Progress for Black individuals and the Black community has frequently been slow. Under the yearbook photo of Harry Case Jr. was the caption "Surmounting all obstacles"[59], which recognized that he faced significant challenges during his time at Phillipsburg High School. Despite the challenges that tested the local Black community over two and a half centuries, individuals came to Phillipsburg and then persuaded relatives and friends from distant states to join them here.

Since the overwhelming majority of Phillipsburg's Black population are descended from 20th century arrivals to the town, few residents, Black or white, have known or been able to pass along the Black threads of Phillipsburg's history. Therefore, the facts and stories of Phillipsburg early Black residents have been unpublished and largely unknown. The information in the appendicies brings together for the first time documentary evidence (almost entirely unavailable online) about the first 130 years of Black history in the town. The census extracts illustrate the ebb and flo of the Black community as people from other states arrive and disappear. Those extracts also show how occupations changed over time.

I do not know and could never include the entirety of the Black experience in Phillipsburg. My hope is that this publication enlarges the definition of who is a Phillipsburger and that it serves as a catalyst for conversation and understanding across our community.

---

[59]   Phillipsburg High School Yearbook, 1929.

Appendix A

Births

Baptisms at St. James Lutheran (Straw) Church

Bap 15 Sept 1788   Susanna   d/Richmond & wife Jane
Born-6/29/1787   both slaves of Valentine Bidelman

Bap 21 June 1789   Catarina   d/Ore & wife Elisabeth
Born-10/31/1787   in Elisabeth Mehlig's house

Baptisms at Old Greenwich Presbyterian Church
20 Nov 1809 (adult)   Betty   G. Bidleman's Black woman

Kennedy Family Bible[60]

Black Phebe	b- 11 Sep 1796	d-26 Dec 1885
Black Dan	b- 27 Mar 1803	
Black Harry	b- 21 Feb 1806	
Black Isabel	b- 20 Dec 1807	
Black Joseph	b- 9 Jan 1820	
Black Ann	b- 8 Jul 1823	

Governmentally Recorded New Jersey Births[61]

Freeman, Sarah E.	d/Martin & Rachel	1 May 1874
Freeman, Stella	d/ Martin & Rachel	18 Apr 1876
Freeman, Hector	s/Martin & Harriet	15 Jan 1870
Freeman, dau	d/Martin & Harriet	3 Apr 1865
Freeman, George	s/Martin & Harriet	7 Jan 1876

---

[60]   Cited by Peggy Warne chapter of the Daughters of the American Revolution in their column "You and History," published in the *Washington Star* in response to an article on December 15, 1960 "Slavery Was Never an Important Institution in Warren County"

[61]   New Jersey, Births and Christenings Index, 1660-1931

Births by Enslaved Women in Greenwich Township[62]

3 June 1806	George Bidleman, Esq.	Samuel Dillyent
3 Oct 1811	Geo. Bidleman, Esq	Clarry
6 June 1817	Henry Bidleman	William
1 July 1815	Henry Bidleman	Ann
25 Sept 1813	Henry Bidleman	Jane
	all 3 children of Darcey & Nathaniel	
10 Aug 1808	Henry Bidleman	Jess
		s/Jemima & Pomp
2 Feb 1813	George Boyer	James
		s/Hetty
12 May 1805	Charles Carter	George
16 Feb 1811	William Carter	Dine d/Phebe
1 Jan 1808	Elizabeth Hibler	Charlotte
21 March 1805	Elizabeth Hibler	Levi Albright
20 Jan 1814	Harbert Hiner	Charles s/Lilla
10 Jun 1809	Isaac Hughes	Nelson s/Bett
28 Nov 1806	Isaac Hughes	Daniel s/Bett
4 July 1806	J. S. Hughes	Clarissa
31 July 1804	Nancy Hughes	Sarah d/Phebe
1 Sept 1808	Robert Innes, Sr	Jack
11 Aug 1806	Robert Innes, Sr	George
21 Feb 1806	Thomas Kennedy	Harry s/Dine
4 May 1806	Robert Kennedy	Dave s/Dine
1 Feb 1813	William Kennedy	Dans s/Rachel
26 Sept 1812	William Kennedy	Joseph
14 Nov 1820	John McKinney	unnamed girl
6 Dec 1823	John William Smith	Joseph
		s/ Lucretia (called Luce)
17 Dec 1812	Thomas Stewart	Hannah
14 Feb 1811	Thomas Stewart	Simon s/Dine

---

[62]   Excerpted from "Warren and Sussex Counties Slave Births" Genealogical Magazine of New Jersey, Vol 54, Nos. 2/3 May/ Sept 1979

Appendix B

19th Century Marriages in Phillipsburg or of Phillipsburg's Black Residents

Married at Trinity Episcopal in Easton[63]
30 Nov 1844	Francis Waterhouse &	Isabella Benjamin
25 Mar 1848	Jacob Prime &	Susannah Groves
28 Jan 1850	Charles Green &	Mary Innes

Married at St. John's Lutheran in Easton
14 May 1831	Abraham James &	Catherine Case
1 Mar 1849	Henry Prime	s/Daniel & Mary
	Sarah Furman	d/Wm & Phoebe Furman

Married at First Colored Lutheran in Easton
26 Jul 1863	Thomas Duncan & Sophia More
24 Jan 1866	Thomas Duncan & Charlotte Freeman

Married at First Presbyterian in Easton
29 Jun 1864	James Spruell & Dianna Jane DeMott
27 Feb 1879	Isaac Malley & Anna J. DeMott

Married at First Methodist in Easton
29 Oct 1852	George Evans &	Margaret Firman
31 Oct 1858	Francis Duncan &	Rachel Freeman
1 Dec 1869	James W. Wilson &	Matilda Smith
30 Nov 1871	Charles H. Holmes &	Henrietta E. Wells

Married at St. Luke's Episcopal in Phillipsburg[64]
30 Jun 1885	Charles Burr & Mary Elizabeth Fox

---

[63] The records for Trinity and the other four Easton churches cited here were transcribed in 1936 by Works Progress Administration workers at Easton Public Library in 1936

[64] Recorded in parish register of St. James Episcopal, Hackettstown

Marriages in New Jersey Records[65]

5 June 1889   Henry Martin & Carrie Freeman   Paper Mill

15 Apr 1896   Spencer Duncan & Carolinda Folks

Married at First Methodist in Phillipsburg[66]

11 Oct 1887   Isaac Warfield & Harriet Prime

11 Aug 1888   James F. Smith & Minnie Prime

11 Sep 1894   Augustus A'vant s/Aug. & Eliz. Bradley

    & Sadie Wilson d/E. H. & M. E. Chamberlin

25 Apr 1896   William Scott   s/Wm & Susan Griffin

    & Julia Hoff   d/Geo & Harriet Prime

Married at Asbury Methodist[67]

3 Oct 1861 James Furman s/ William & Phebe   Stewartsville

    & Anna James d/ Abraham & Catherine   Bloomsbury

Married at Stewartsville Lutheran [68]

29 Dec 1879   J. B. Hogan & Anna A. Burr

Marriages in Warren County Records[69]

30 Oct 1830 Robert Miller & Effie Dunken   P. Fine, Jr, JP

        (people of colour)

13 Feb 1834 Aaron O. Hoff & Dinah Boston   Rev. Candee

        (free colored people)

2 Oct 1841 Thomas Duncan (colored man) & Eunice Osmun

24 Aug 1844 Martin Freeman & Effie Miller M. Hulshizer, JP

---

[65]   *New Jersey Marriage Records 1670-1965*

[66]   Gangeware, Beulah, *First Methodist Church, Phillipsburg, NJ*

[67]   O'Brien, John, *Methodist Church Records of the Asbury Circuit*

[68]   Stryker, Katherine *Ev. Lutheran Church of Stewartsville*, 1967

[69]   Smith, Henry *Warren County Marriage Records 1824 -1881*

Marriages in Hunterdon County Records[70]

8 Sep 1860   Martin Freeman & Harriett Martin   by Spoor
22 Feb 1893   Daniel L. Freeman & Mary L. Hackett
Bloomsbury
3 Apr 1897   Edward Freeman & Frances Groves
Bloomsbury

Marriages in Morris County[71]

1 Jan 1862   Alexander Bidleman & Margaret Jane Valentine
1 Jan 1862   Alex Bidleman & Margaret Ballentine in Mendham
1 Jan 1862   Hezekiah Bidleman & Charlotte S. Ray
4 Jul 1867   Hezekiah Bidleman & Elizabeth Jackson
                            in Chatham
9 Apr 1883   Hezekiah Bridleman & Lelia Watson in Newark

---

[70]   Deats, Hiram, *Marriage Records of Hunterdon County 1795-1875*
[71]   *New Jersey Marriage Records 1670-1965*

Appendix C

Greenwich Township Manumissions

16 Dec 1847	Robert Kennedy	Betty Bird	
20 Sept 1833	William P. Roberson	Harry Pursel	39yr
29 Mar 1833	Lewis Kline	Betty	28yr
11 Jan 1833	Col. Jonathan Robins	Susan	29yr
18 Mar 1831	Philip Weller estate	James	27yr
12 Jan 1829	Robert Kennedy	Hettie	37yr
28 Jan 1829	Thomas Kennedy	Dan Coacher	26yr
20 Feb 1826	William Budd Smith	Phebe	36yr
26 Dec 1825	Abraham Arndt	Philice	28yr
26 Dec 1825	Abraham Arndt	Joseph	31yr
26 Dec 1825	Jacob Arndt	Jake	38yr
23 May 1825	John & Philip Weller	Nathaniel	21-40yr
11 Mar 1824	John W. Smith	Lucretia (Luce)	24yr
10 Apr 1824	Thomas Kennedy	Phebe	27yr
10 Dec 1822	Michael Roseberry	Sarah	28yr
4 Dec 1815	William Kennedy	Rachel	
26 Mar 1812	George Bidleman	Betty	

Oxford Township Manumission

17 Sept 1818	Rev. Garner A. Hunt	Betty Mingo Firman	24yr

Hunterdon County manumissions

12 Oct 1816	Rev. William B. Sloan	Simon
5 Jul 1817	Henry Waterhouse estate	Frank
17 Apr 1824	Rev. William B. Sloan	Aaron

Slaves mentioned in Greenwich Township estates

1786	Edward Hunt	Sambo
1807	John Schooley	Joe
1808	George Geassar	Pompey
1809	Peter Wyckoff	negro wench (unnamed)
1810	Robert Kennedy	Dave, Dian, Joe, Silva
1812	Philip Weller	Tone
1813	Thomas Barber	negro girl (unnamed)
1825	John S. Hughes	Betsy, Matty

Manumission of Sarah by Michael Roseberry

State of New Jersey, Sussex County to wit   We do certify that on this tenth day of December in the year of our Lord eighteen hundred and twenty two Michael Roseberry of the Township of Greenwich in the county of Sussex brought before us two of the overseers of the poor of the said township and two of the justices of the peace of the said county his slave named "Sarah" who on view and examination appears to us to be sound in mind and not under any bodily incapacity of obtaining a support and also is not under the age of twenty one years nor above the age of forty years In witness whereof we have hereunto set our hands the day and year above written Philip Fine and Barnet Dewitt, Overseers of the Poor
John Carpenter and Rob't D. Stewart, Justices of the Peace

State of New Jersey To all whom these presents shall come greeting, It is hereby made known that on this tenth day of December in the year of our Lord Eighteen hundred and twenty two, I Michael Roseberry of the Township of Greenwich in the county of Sussex have liberated, manumitted and set free my Negroe slave called "Sarah" of the age of twenty eight years or thereabouts and I do hereby liberate, manumit and set free my said slave and discharge her from all services or demand of service to be hereafter made either by me or by any person claiming by from or under me. In testimony whereof I set my hand and seal the day and year above written and delivered in the presence of us. Philip Fine Jun'r__Rob't D. Stewart
Michael Roseberry

State of New Jersey, Sussex County
Be it remembered that on the tenth day of December in the year of our Lord Eighteen hundred and twenty two personally came before me, Thomas Stewart, one of the judges of the court of common pleas of Sussex county aforesaid, Michael Roseberry the grantor of the above instrument of manumission who did acknowledge that he sealed and delivered the said instrument of manumission for the uses and purpose therein mentioned. Taken before me   Tho Stewart
Rec'd and recorded 26 December 1822

Appendix D

Census Extracts

1790 Census – Greenwich Township
64 Slaves

1800 Census – Greenwich township
census lost

1810 Census – Greenwich Township
census lost

1820 Census – Greenwich Township
14 male slaves   17 female slaves
23 free Black males   18 free Black females

1830 Census – Greenwich Township
6 male slaves   9 female slaves
25 free Black males   27 free Black females

1840 Census – Greenwich Township
1 male slave
39 free Black males   32 free Black females

1830 Census

Slaveowners

Carter, Chas, Esq	1 M	24-35
Cline, Jacob	1 F	24-35
Cline, William	1 F	24-35
Fair, John	1 F	24-35
Feit, Paul	1 M	36-55
Heiner, Herbert	2 F	10-23, 56-99
Kennedy, Robert H	2 M	10-23, 56-99
Kline, John	1 F	10-23
Overly, John	1 F	36-55
Robbins, John S.	1 F	10-23
Robbins, Jonathan	1 F	24-35
Snyder, Henry	1 M	24-35
Weller, Samuel	1 M	24-35

Free Black Households

Demut, Thomas	2 M	<10, 36-55
	1 F	24-35
Emery, Joseph	1 M	24-35
	3 F	(2)<10, 24-35
Firman, William	1 M	10-23
	3 F	(2)<10, 10-23
Sloan, Simon	2 M	<10, 36-55
	3 F	(2) 10-23, 36-55

1830 Census (continued)

White Households with Free Black Residents

Brakeley, George	1 M	10-23
Carpenter, George	1 F	<10
Carpenter, Joseph A.	1 F	10-23
Carpenter, Joseph B.	1 M	<10
Carpenter, Maria (wid)	1 F	24-35
Cooper, Benjamin	1 F	10-23
Cougle, Peter	1 M	24-35
Creveling, Jacob	1 F	10-23
Creveling, William	1 F	10-23
Gardner, Joseph	1 F	24-35
Hamlin, John	1 M	10-23
Houghawort, Leford	1 M	10-23
Hughes, Hugh	1 M	36-55
Kennedy, James J.	2 M	(2) 10-23
Kennedy, Phineas B.	1 F	<10
Kennedy, Robert S.	1 M	10-23
Kennedy, William, Esq	1 F	10-23
Muirhead, Wm	1 M	10-23
Piat, John	1 M	10-23
Pursel, John	2 M	<10, 10-23
	1 F	24-35
Shipman, Isaac	1 M	10-23
Sloan, Wm. B.	1 M	10-23
	2 F	10-23, 36-55
Smith, John	1 M	24-35
Stiles, Jacob	1 M	24-35
	2 F	(2) 10-23
Stewart, Rob't D.	1 F	10-23
Tinsman, Christian	1 F	24-35
Weller, Samuel	2 M	(2)<10
	1 F	24-35

1840 Census – Greenwich Township

Free Black Households males   females
Dunkon, Joseph   1 <10, 1 24-35   1<10, 1 24-35
Bray, Michael   1 10-23, 1 36-54   1 10-23, 1 36-54
Robeson, Samuel   2 <10, 1 36-54   1 24-35, 1 55-99
Heagon, Aaron   2 <10, 1 36-54   2 <10, 1 36-54
James, Abraham   3 <10, 1 24-35   1 24-35
Motison, Richard   1 24-35   1 24-35
Burr, James   1 36-54   1 36-54
Furman, William   Males   2 <10, 1 10-23, 1 24-35, 1 36-54
                        Females   1 <10, 2 10-23, 1 36-54
Emery, Joseph   2 <10, 1 10-23, 1 36-54   1 24-35
Demut, Thomas 1 <10, 1 10-23, 1 36-54 1 10-23, 1 36-54, 1 55-99
Innis, John   1 24-35   2 <10, 1 10-23, 1 24-35

White Households with Free Black residents
Staats, John   1 10-24
Robbins, Jonathon   1 24-35
Haughwort, Leffert   1 24-35
Kennedy, Robert 1 24-35
Hulshizer, Martin   1 10-23
Smith, John W.   1 10-23   1 24-35
Hunt, Samuel   1 10-23
Sitgreaves, Charles   1 24-35
Stewart, William   1 10-23
Hines, Isaac   1 100+
Arndt, Abram   1 10-23
Arndt, Jacob   1 10-23
Carpenter, Joseph B.   1 10-23
Carpenter, Mary Elizabeth   1 100+
Fine, Philip   1 24-35
David Dunken   1 10-23

One Household still owned a slave
Snyder, Henry   1 55-99

1850 Census -- Greenwich

Name	Age	Birth	Occupation	RE
Carter, Daniel	47	NJ	laborer	$200
" Rachel	40	PA		
Furman, Phoebe	55	NJ		$200
" Abraham	20	NJ	laborer	
" Henry	18	NJ		
" James	17	NJ	in school	
" Mary M.	16	NJ		
Jones, Thos. J.	59	NJ	laborer	
Haughabout, Hetty	18	NJ		
Hageman, Jonathan	12	NJ		
James, Abraham	39	NJ	laborer	$300
" Catharine	34	NJ		
" Alfred	17	NJ		
" Moses	15	NJ	in school	
" William	11	NJ	in school	
" George	8	NJ	in school	
" Ann	5	NJ		
" Elizabeth	3	NJ		
DeMott, Thos.	50	NJ	hostler	$1200
" Jane	38	NJ		
" Henry	22	NJ		
" Anna	5	NJ		
Freeman, Rachel	15	NJ		
Burr, Henry	33	NJ	laborer	
" Caroline	34	NJ		
" Henry H.	7	NJ		
" Louise I.	4	NJ		
" William K.	3m	NJ		
Duncan, Joseph	38	NJ	hostler	
" Catharine	32	NJ		
" Frank	12	NJ		
" Thomas		NJ	in school	
Freeman, Dotty Ann	17	NJ		
Russell, James	38	NJ	laborer	
" Martha	26	NJ		
Oliver, George	19	NJ	laborer	

Emery, Charlotte	44	NJ		
" Enoch	23	NJ		
" Mary	21	NJ		
" Margaret	19	NJ		
" Norris	16	NJ		
" John J.	15	NJ		
" Junior	9	NJ	in school	
Miller, James	23	NJ	Jacob Hulshizer's farm	
Miller, Thos.	13	NJ	William Carpenter's farm	
Miller, Robert	20	NJ	Joseph Carpenter's farm	
Sloan, Sarah	12	NJ	Joseph Carpenter's farm	
Bidelman, Isacher	13	NJ	John Pursel's farm	
Innes, John	49	NJ	laborer	
" Mary	46	NJ		
" Hetti	15	NJ		
" Lucy	1	NJ		
Grandin, Mary	8	NJ	w/Thomas Hunt family	
Freeman, Martin	34	NJ	laborer	
" Euphemia	41	NJ		
" Henrietta	7	NJ	school	
" Martin	5	NJ		
" Bray	3	NJ		
" Joseph	1	NJ		
" Spencer	11	NJ		
Miller, John	14	NJ	on Joseph Hughes farm	
Freeman, Charlotte	14	NJ	on Joseph Hughes farm	
Harris, Margaret	10	NJ	w/William & Eliz. Harris	
Miller, George	40	NJ	laborer	
Waterhouse, Francis	38	NJ	laborer	$200
" Isabella	40	NJ		
Beidelman, John	65	NJ	laborer	
" Hetty	45	NJ		
" Alexander	15	NJ		
" Hezekiah	14	NJ		
" Lani	8	NJ		
" John	4	NJ		
" William	3	NJ		
" Martha	2	NJ		
" Ackey	2m	NJ		

1860 Census – Phillipsburg

Name		Age	Birth	Occupation	RE
DeMott,	Thomas	65	NJ	hostler	$1500
"	, Jane	44	NJ		
"	Ann	15	NJ		
Welsh,	Robert	35	NY	barber	
"	Sidney	20	PA		
"	Charles	2	NJ		
"	James	3m	NJ		
Black,	Sidney	23	NJ	servant – hotel	
Black,	Rhodes C.	28	PA	barber	
"	Marion	23	PA		
Prime,	Daniel	17	PA	barber	
Rosin,	James	42	VA	waiter	
"	Patty	37	NJ	cook	
Truax,	Nelson	25	PA	hostler	
Duncan,	Joseph	50	NJ	hostler	
Dunmore,	Edward	35	PA	laborer	
"	Debby	30	NJ		
"	Mary	4	NJ		
"	William	6	NJ		
"	Sarah	3	NJ		
"	Edward	2m	NJ		
Chamberlin,	Mahlon	35	NJ	laborer	
"	Christina	30	NJ		
"	May Ellen	15	NJ		
"	George	11	PA		
"	Matilda	3	PA		
Symes,	Benjamin	27	NJ	laborer	
"	Mary B.	19	NJ		
Johnson,	Samuel	40	NJ	laborer	
"	Catherine	21	NJ		
"	Mary	1	NJ		
Forman,	Jane	40	NJ	wash woman	
"	Adam	22	NJ	waiter	
"	Dewilliam	16	NJ	laborer	
"	James	14	NJ		

Johnson,	Thomas	39	PA	hostler
Black,	Daniel	25	unk	teamster
Duncan,	Frank	20	NJ	laborer
"	Marian	21	NJ	
"	Alice	8m	NJ	
Miller,	Mary	15	NJ	servant
Innes,	Charles H.	48	NJ	laborer
"	Martha	35	NJ	
"	Joseph	1	NJ	
Provost,	Susan	60	NJ	

1860 Census– Greenwich Township

Burr,	Samuel	24	NJ	laborer	
"	Jane	22	NJ		
Miller,	Thomas	22	NJ	farm laborer	
Innes,	John	54	NJ	laborer	
"	Mary	52	NJ		
"	Lucinda	13	NJ	in school	
"	William	8	NJ	in school	
"	L. Francis	6	NJ	in school	
Huff,	Nelson	31	NJ	farm laborer	
"	Hager	33	NJ		
"	Susan	8	NJ	in school	
"	Amanda	5	NJ	in school	
Furman,	James	19	NJ	farm laborer	
McQuarter,	Daniel	57	NJ	laborer	
"	Rachel	40	PA		
Forman,	Abraham	27	NJ	farm laborer	
Miller,	George	50	NJ	laborer w/Dr. Isaac Stewart	
Waterhouse,	Frances	50	NJ	laborer	$450
"	Isabella	50	NJ		
Forman,	Phoebe	58	NJ	wash woman	$200

James,	Abraham	50	NJ	laborer	$200
Robins,	Dianah	50	NJ		
James,	William	20	NJ	laborer	
"	George	17	NJ	laborer	
"	Anna	16	NJ		
"	Elizabeth	15	NJ		
Freeman,	Martin	50	NJ	laborer	$500
"	Charlotte	25	NJ		
"	Martin	15	NJ	in school, laborer	
"	Joseph	10	NJ	in school	
"	Isaac	8	NJ	in school	
"	Emaline	6	NJ	in school	
"	Alice	5	NJ		
"	Alfred	2	NJ		
Miller,	Robert	30	NJ	Philip Reese farm	
Miller,	John	12	NJ	in school	
Freeman,	Bray	12	NJ	in school	w/Jonas Brooks

1870 Census – Phillipsburg

Name		Age	Birth	Occupation	RE
Lambert,	George	44	NJ	cook	
Duncan,	Joseph	55	NJ	laborer	
"	Catherine	59	NJ		
"	George C.	18	NJ	laborer	
"	Sallie	13	NJ		
"	Kate	10	NJ		
"	Agnes	7	NJ		
"	Christiana	35	NJ		
DeMot,	Thomas	70	NJ	laborer	$1200
"	Jane	50	NJ		
Stephens,	Irene	8	NJ		
Spruel,	Ann J.	27	NJ		
"	James K.	3	NJ		
"	Emory	3m	NJ		
Teneike,	Elijah	38	NJ	laborer	
Braxton,	Hannah	22	NJ		
Anderson,	Elias	70	PA	hostler	
Chamberlin,	Kate	8	NJ		
Wells,	Henry	51	NJ	laborer	$500
"	Susan	29	NJ		
"	Henrietta	17	NJ		
"	George	8	NJ	school	
"	Charles	5	NJ		
"	William	2	NJ		
Vaneiken,	Mary	63	NJ		

1880 – Phillipsburg

Exton,	William	66	NJ	laborer
"	Martha	46	NJ	keep house
"	Mansfield	25	NJ	coachman
"	Josephine	19	NJ	sewing
Price,	Susan	34	NJ	domestic
Jefferson,	Frances	26	NJ	domestic
Steppler,	Elizabeth	45	NJ	washing
"	Martha	18	NJ	washing
"	William	12	NJ	
Robinson,	Charles	31	MD	hostler
"	Anna	31	NJ	keep house
Duncan,	George	28	PA	laborer
"	Henrietta	24	NJ	keep house
DeMott,	Jane	65	NJ	washing
Smalley,	Isaac	51	NJ	laborer
"	Anna	35	NJ	washing
"	James	11	NJ	school
Chamberlain,	Malon	60	NJ	laborer
"	Christiana	56	NJ	keep house
"	Sarah	23	PA	washing
"	Catherine	19	NJ	washing
"	Agnes	16	NJ	washing
Benjamin,	Daniel	45	NJ	laborer
Benjamin,	Elizabeth	72	PA	keep house

1900 Census - Phillipsburg

Smith,	Frank	31	VA	RR Dining car steward
" ,	Martha	28	VA	Servant
A'Vant,	Augustus	46	NC	Foundry laborer
" ,	Sadie	27	PA	
" ,	Augustus	2	PA	
" ,	Ethel	1	PA	
Hackett,	William	25	NJ	Cement mill laborer
" ,	Lucy	24	VA	
" ,	Keylcee	3	NJ	
" ,	Warren	2	NJ	
Duncan,	Spencer	33	PA	Hostler
" ,	Caroline	21	VA	
" ,	Henry	3	NJ	
" ,	Agnes	1	NJ	
Chamberlain,	Robert	22	NJ	Ice wagon laborer
Johnson,	Wesley	37	DE	Servant (domestic)
" ,	Elizabeth	33	DE	Servant (domestic)
Rich,	John M.	35	PA	Servant (domestic)
Crawford,	Charles	30	NY	Servant (domestic)
" ,	Sarah	28	NY	Servant (domestic)
Fell,	Sarah	40	PA	Servant (domestic)
Hortman,	Joseph	35	NJ	RR Dining car waiter
" ,	Alice	30	VA	
" ,	Mannie	12	NJ	at school
Jackson,	Susan	17	VA	Servant (domestic)
" ,	Patty	17	VA	Servant (domestic)
Davis,	Mary	31	VA	Laundress
Washington,	George	53	NC	Cement mill laborer
Burr,	Arthur	31	NJ	Porter
" ,	Mary	28	VA	
Outen,	Cornelius	21	VA	Boilermaker
Frame,	Alvin	16	PA	Laborer

1910 Census – Phillipsburg

Hager,	Jennie	26	NJ	House servant
Wilson,	Jennie	36	NJ	Laborer
"	Annabelle	18	NJ	Laborer
"	Oscar	16	NJ	Pipe foundry
"	Dewey	12	NJ	
"	Asher	8	NJ	
"	Bernice	5	NJ	
"	Herman	3	NJ	
Hackett,	William	34	NJ	Pipe foundry
Freeman,	Daniel	32	NJ	Pipe foundry
"	Mary	29	NJ	
"	Florence	17	NJ	servant
"	Martin	16	NJ	
"	Viola	12	NJ	
Hackett,	Nathan	68	NJ	
"	Lydia	56	NJ	
Smith,	Sarah	23	NJ	
Lewis,	Bessie	14	NJ	kitchen servant
Spahn,	Emily	18	NJ	kitchen servant
Freeman,	Elizabeth	25	NJ	kitchen servant
Burr,	Arthur	41	NJ	Boiler works
"	Ella	31	VA	
Munroe,	Charles	28	MA	Boiler works
"	Anna	26	VA	
"	Evert	8	MA	
"	Warren	7	MA	
"	Lillian	34m	MA	
"	Corneliss	16m	MA	
Freeman,	George	28	NJ	Boiler works
"	Lillian	29	NJ	

Dickerson,	Daniel	39	VA	Hod carrier
"	Missie	29	VA	
"	Grace	15	VA	
"	Roena	12	NJ	
"	Lavinia	10	NJ	
"	Levi	8	NJ	
"	Clarence	6	NJ	
"	Frank	3	NJ	
"	William Taft	14m	NJ	
Waller,	Ferd	25	NJ	Odd jobs
Dickerson,	Richard	39	VA	Pipe foundry
"	Hattie L.	35	VA	
"	Seabury E.	17	VA	Pipe foundry
"	Alton W.	12	NJ	
"	Richard E. Jr	10	NJ	
"	Ethel G.	7	NJ	
"	James	1	NJ	
Frame,	Alvin	26	PA	
Rosser,	William	38	VA	Pipe foundry
"	Thennie	37	VA	
"	William J.	15	NJ	Pipe foundry
"	Lemmie	14	NJ	
"	Cassie	11	NJ	
"	Mary	10	NJ	
"	Irene	6	NJ	
"	Albert	4	NJ	
"	Edward	2	NJ	
"	Lewis	2m	NJ	
Washington,	George	60	NC	Cement mill
"	Nettie	40	VA	
Parker,	Sarah	41	VA	Cook
West,	Peachy	24	VA	Waitress
Marshall,	George	35	DC	Laborer odd jobs
"	Louisa M.	24	VA	

1920 Census – Phillipsburg

Freeman,	Theodore	42	NJ	Coal wagon driver
"	Caroline	15	NJ	
"	Paul	10	NJ	
Hortman,	Joseph B.	58	NJ	Elks Club steward
"	Alice C.	59	VA	
Wyckoff,	Mary E.	30	NJ	Servant
Freeman,	Daniel	45	NJ	Foundry
"	Mary	42	NJ	
"	Florence	25	NJ	Dressmaker
"	Martin	23	NJ	Waiter – hotel
McClary,	Viola	21	NJ	
Hackett,	Nathan	78	NJ	
Haymer,	William	22	PA	Machinist shop
Martin,	Hilda	22	PA	Servant
Martin,	James	27	NJ	Foundry laborer
"	Anna	24	NJ	
"	Mildred	7	NJ	in school
"	Carolyn	1 9/12	NJ	
Freeman,	Lillian	40	VA	Seamstress
Frame,	Alvin	36	PA	Foundry laborer
Burr,	Arthur V.	51	NJ	Stationary Engineer
"	Mary E.	49	VA	
Camp,	Arthur	38	GA	Railroad laborer
Haines,	Lucy	42	PA	housekeeper
Steel,	Sara	40	NJ	Cook YMCA
"	Bertha	33	NJ	Servant YMCA
"	Thelma	8	NJ	
"	Mary	5	NJ	
Chamberlin,	Robert L.	39	NJ	Machinist – Steel Works
"	Jennie T.	39	NJ	
"	Jane	2 4/12	NJ	

1930 Census – Phillipsburg

Squires,	George W.	53	PA	cook – Steam RR
"	Carrie L.	34	SC	
"	Catherine E.	6	NJ	in school
Robinson,	Charles E.	42	WA[72]	laborer -odd jobs
"	Arvilla	26	NJ	
Wallace,	Esau	38	SC	laborer - telephone co.
"	Rebekah	41	SC	
"	Rose M.	9	SC	in school
"	Ruth E.	8	SC	in school
"	Anna R.	3	NJ	
Johnson,	James	29	VA	laborer – hospital
"	Mary E.	34	DC	
"	Alice M.	19	MA	
"	James J.	18	MD	laborer – hospital
"	Martha	3	PA	
Carter,	Lewis	32	VA	laborer – foundry
"	Lucy	24	VA	
Freeman,	Lillian V.	50	VA	dressmaker
Lear,	Gladys E.	28	PA	
Johnson,	Jessie	19	NJ	servant
Carter,	James	49	VA	laborer for contractor
"	Susie	56	VA	
Frame,	Alvin	47	PA	cement laborer
Burr,	Arthur	60	NJ	boiler works – stat. engr.
"	Mary	58	VA	
Fowler,	William M.	48	SC	laborer – odd jobs
'	Bula	39	SC	
Black,	Boyd	35	SC	
Gregory,	William H.	29	VA	cement plant laborer
"	Maggie L.	27	VA	
Hoskins,	Rufus L.	44	VA	odd jobs
Booker,	Dora	38	VA	servant in restaurant
Threets,	Elizabeth	15	VA	
Baxter,	Charles	65	GA	cook in hospital

---

[72] In other census records Charles' birth is listed as Maryland

Appendix E

Deaths and Burials

Phillipsburg Deaths in NJ records

Emery, Joseph	May 1850	54	M
Chamberlain, Mahlon	12 Apr 1881	63	M
Benjamin, Eliz.	24 Jun 1882	80	Wd
Exton, Josephine	21 Feb 1885	25 4m	S
Cooper, Fannie E.	16 May 1886	1 11m	
Smith, Lydia	21 Dec 1885	40	S
Coogan, Michael	14 Jun 1887	19	
Exton, Wm. H.	23 Jan 1887	31 4m	S
Fuller, David	2 Jan 1888	25	S
Lyle, Katie	18 Apr 1892	30	M
Wilson, Clarence M.	20 Apr 1889	4 10m	
Lum, Benj.	24 Mar 1890	48	M
Lockley, Hazel	24 Sep 1893	1	
Robbins, Gertrude	13 Sep 1893	45	M
Vangeason, Zachariah	16 May 1894	17	S
Simes, Gardner	27 Apr 1896	12	
Exton, Martha	22 Sep 1895	61 9m	M
Lyle, John	12 Nov 1896	48	S

Local Civil War soldiers burials

Bidleman, Alexander   1911 Evergreen Cem, Morristown, NJ
Bidleman, Hezekiah 14 Aug 1925 Cypress Hills Nat'l Cem,
                                          Brooklyn, NY
Duncan, Frank   29 Apr 1920 Baptist cemetery Burlington, NJ
Duncan, Thomas 14 Jun 1915 Greenwich Pres, Cem.,
Hackett, Nathan   17 Feb 1920   Phillipsburg Cem.
James, Alfred 11 Oct 1864 City Point Nat'l Cem, Hopewell, VA
Prime, Daniel   17 Jul 1921   Easton Heights Cem., Easton, PA
Spruell, James   1 Jul 1889
Truax, Nelson   19 Oct 1909 Beverly Nat'l Cem, Beverly, NJ

Deaths in Easton Records

First Colored Lutheran in Easton

Sophia Duncan   b-1 Feb 1846
                  d-26 Apr 1864   int-Colored Cem.
Francis Martin Duncan s/Francis & Rachel
b-14 Apr 1864   d-15 Aug 1864   int-Colored Cem.
Jenny Ann Spruell   d/James & Ann
b-7 Apr 1865   d-27 Jun 1866   int 1st Pres Cem
Josephine Duncan d/Francis & Rachel   b-14 Oct 1862
                  d-31 Mar 1866
Sanford Duncan   s/Francis & Rachel b-13 Mar 1866
                  d-2 Apr 1866
Louisa Benjamin   of Phillipsburg   int-1 Jun 1871
Elias Anderson   d-26 Feb 1882   int-1 Mar 1882 Easton Cem.

First Presbyterian in Easton

Edward F. Spruell   s/James & Ann
b-11 Sep 1863   d-13 Feb 1869   int 1st Pres Cem
Thomas DeMott   d-20 Sep 1872

Easton Express Death Notice
Emory C. Spruell   s/James & Ann   d-4 Dec 1871   age 1y

Black Burials in Straw Church Cemetery

John Innis   b- 1 Sep 1808   d- 7 Nov 1883

Feit, John estate Section 9, Plot 56, Grave C
Feit farm sold to Ingersoll Rand Co. Bodies of 11 slaves
removed by Jacob Feit from the old Feit cemetery on this farm
11-2-1902. $2.00 Paid for interment.
Copied from cemetery records by Midge Covert

Black Burials in Phillipsburg Cemetery (to 1920)

Avant, Augustus	28 Sep 1908	54
Exton, Josephine	21 Feb 1885	25y 4m
Exton, Martha	22 Sep 1895	61
Exton, William	23 Jan 1887	31
Hackett, Nathan	17 Feb 1920	78
Hackett, Kelsey	18 Dec 1900	4y
Hackett, Lucy	9 Mar 1903	24
Hackett, Warren	12 Nov 1900	3y
Lockley, Hazel	24 Sep 1893	24d
Spruell, James K.	4 Aug 1893	35
Unnamed child	1844	
Washburn, Ruth	29 Nov 1912	29.4.16
Washington, George	11 Apr 1917	55.11.29

Black Burials in Easton Cemetery

Elias Anderson		I- 1 Mar 1882
Mahlon Chamberlin	68	I-15 Apr 1881
Christianna Chamberlin	78	I-18 Dec 1906
George W. Chamberlin	51	I- 9 Jan 1913
Agnes D. Lee	44	I-11 Feb 1908
Walter T. Lee	1	I-20 May 1895
Minnie M. Lee	2	I-22 Feb 1886
Alice Lee	1	I-16 Aug 1884
John Lyle	48	I-14 Nov 1896
Katie Lyle	30	I-20 Apr 1892
John N. Lyle	stillborn	I- 5 Jul 1888
Sarah C. Ross	67	I-17 Jun 1924

Death Certificate of Christianna Chamberlin

Appendix F

Property Transactions

28 Apr 1837 Thomas Demott from Peter Skillman for $500.00
    property in Phillipsburg along New Jersey Turnpike
15 Dec 1863 Thomas DeMott to Morris & Essex RR $1800.00
    property in Phillipsburg along New Jersey Turnpike
23 Dec 1863 Thomas DeMott from Henry Segreaves $700.00
    property on east side of Randall street
11 Apr 1874 Mortgage of property by Thomas Demott
11 Apr 1877 Mortgage on property by Thomas DeMott
11 Sep 1888 Sheriff's sale of property of Jane DeMott
    to satisfy debt of $524.93

22 Jun 1839 Will of William B. Sloan
"I give and devise unto Abraham, the colored man who works for
me, to his heirs and assigns the house where he now lives."

3 Apr 1840 Abraham James to John W. Smith for $5.00
    property inherited by will of Rev. William B. Sloan
3 Apr 1840 John W. Smith to Abraham James for $5.00
25 Mar 1859 Abraham James to Alfred James for $500.00
    property on Greenwich Tp adjacent to William Smith's land

24 Mar 1849 Francis Waterhouse from estate of Philip Fine
    property in Greenwich Tp

6 Feb 1858 Martin Freeman from John & Charity Sinclair
$90.00   property in Greenwich Tp

25 Nov 1868 Henry Wells from Joseph Howell for $176.00
    property in Phillipsburg between Spruce & Cedar
16 Jun 1874 Sheriff's sale of property of Henry Wells
    to satisfy debt of $1120.00

For Further Reading

Geffken, Rick, *Stories of Slavery in New Jersey*
Charleston, SC: The History Press, 2021.

Gilby, Joseph G., *"Freedom to All"*
Hightstown: Longstreet House, 2011.

Hodges, Graham Russell Gae, *Black New Jersey*
New Brunswick: Rutgers University Press, 2019.

Leary, Frank, ed. *Pohatcong: the Prologue*
Pohatcong, NJ: Pohatcong Heritage Commission, 1981.

NJ Underground Railroad Project *Report to the New Jersey Legislature*, Trenton, 2002.

Report of the NJ State Temporary Commission on the Condition of the Urban Colored Population, Trenton, 1939.

Safian, Gail R., *Slavery in New Jersey: A Troubled Past*
Maplewood, NJ: Durand-Hedden House & Garden Ass'n, 2019.

Schwartz, David "Lopatcong" in *History of Sussex and Warren Counties*, compiled by James Snell,
Philadelphia: Everts & Peck, 1881.

Snell, James, ed "Slavery and Servitude in Hunterdon and Somerset" *History of Hunterdon & Somerset Counties, NJ*
Philadelphia: Everts & Peck, 1881.

Switala, William J., Underground Railroad in New York and New Jersey, Mechanicsburg, PA: Stackpole Books, 2006.

Wright, Giles, *Afro-Americans in New Jersey*
Trenton: New Jersey Historical Commission, 1988.

Wright, Giles R. & Wonkeryor, Edward Lama *"Steal Away, Steal Away"* Trenton: New Jersey Historical Commission, 2000.

Index

Slave Index

About the Author

Wayne Calvin Sherrer, born in Phillipsburg, is a sixth generation resident of Phillipsburg, NJ. He is a past president of the Phillipsburg Area Historical Society and research associate of the Warren County Historical and Genealogical Society. His published works include A Guide to Civil War Graves in Phillipsburg Cemetery, transcriptions of the parish records of Wesley Methodist Church and St. Luke's Episcopal Church (both in Phillipsburg) and an article in The Historiographer. He is an Episcopal priest in the Diocese of Newark and an avid genealogist.